Dear Graduate עמו״ש:

   May the love and knowledge of Torah, fostered by your years at HANC, enable you to meet the challenges around you and to kindle the spirits, minds and hearts of those whose paths you cross.

Mazal Tov and Hatzlacha

The Hebrew Academy of Nassau County
and the HANC PTA
2015/5775

ArtScroll® Series

Rabbi Nosson Scherman / Rabbi Meir Zlotowitz
General Editors

A TOUCH

STORIES OF STRENGTH—
THAT LIFT, BUILD
AND ENCOURAGE

Published by

ArtScroll
Mesorah Publications, ltd.

OF CHIZUK

RABBI YECHIEL SPERO

FIRST EDITION
First Impression ... November 2014
Second Impression ... February 2015

Published and Distributed by
MESORAH PUBLICATIONS, LTD.
4401 Second Avenue / Brooklyn, N.Y 11232

Distributed in Europe by
LEHMANNS
Unit E, Viking Business Park
Rolling Mill Road
Jarow, Tyne & Wear, NE32 3DP
England

Distributed in Australia and New Zealand
by **GOLDS WORLDS OF JUDAICA**
3-13 William Street
Balaclava, Melbourne 3183
Victoria, Australia

Distributed in Israel by
SIFRIATI / A. GITLER — BOOKS
Moshav Magshimim
Israel

Distributed in South Africa by
KOLLEL BOOKSHOP
Northfield Centre, 17 Northfield Avenue
Glenhazel 2192, Johannesburg, South Africa

ARTSCROLL® SERIES
A TOUCH OF CHIZUK
© Copyright 2014, by MESORAH PUBLICATIONS, Ltd.
4401 Second Avenue / Brooklyn, N.Y. 11232 / (718) 921-9000 / www.artscroll.com

To contact the author with comments or stories, he can be reached via e-mail
at chiely1@gmail.com

ISBN 10: 1-4226-1543-X / ISBN 13: 978-1-4226-1543-0

Typography by CompuScribe at ArtScroll Studios, Ltd.
Printed in the United States of America by Noble Book Press Corp.
Bound by Sefercraft, Quality Bookbinders, Ltd., Brooklyn N.Y. 11232

ב"ה

י"ג מנחם אב תשס"ג

מכתב ברכה

לכבוד ידידי הרב יחיאל ספירא שליט"א, רבי בישיבת הק'
חפץ חיים בבלטימור,

הנה בא לפני עלים מספרך אשר כתבת ושמו "נתרגש פון א
מעשה" הנה כשמו כן הוא כולו ספורים יקרים המביא
רגשות קודש להקוראים בו, מה שנחוץ זה למאוד לחזק
האמונה וללמוד איך להתנהג באמונה ובמדות טובות כמו
שעולה מהספורים. ולכן אברכהו שיצליח בספרו ושיהנו
הקוראים בו,והשם יתב' יברכהו להרבות תורה ומוסר
ויגדיל תורה ויאדיר.

ממני ידידו המברכו בכל לב

דוד קוויאט

Michtav Berachah written for *Touched by a Story*

ACKNOWLEDGMENTS

I T IS WITH A TREMENDOUS SENSE OF HUMILITY THAT I thank the Al-mighty for everything He has done for my family and for me. It is easy to take things for granted, and too often, we fall into that trap. I hope this note of appreciation shows that in some small way, I am acknowledging that everything I have accomplished comes from Him.

Rabbi Meir Zlotowitz and **Rabbi Nosson Scherman** never treat me like an employee, and I have never looked at them as my bosses. With their vast experience and knowledge, they have guided me during the past 12 years; they are always concerned for my well-being. I trust them fully and treasure their friendship.

My heartfelt thanks to the **ArtScroll staff:**

Gedaliah Zlotowitz — a dependable and reliable friend, who always finds an encouraging word.

Avrohom Biderman — another dear *chaver*, who looks out for what is best for me.

Mendy Herzberg — a great person to work with, who manages to keep his cool, even when things are heating up.

Eli Kroen — a talented artist, who has, once again, captured the essence of the book. Magnificent!

A special note of thanks to **Mrs. Estie Dicker** for paginating so skillfully; **Mrs. Mindy Stern** for touching up the stories and perfecting each one; and **Mrs. Faygie Weinbaum** for her proofreading with such accuracy.

This year, my dear parents, **Dr. and Mrs. Abba and Sarah Spero**, spent Simchas Torah with us. One night, as we walked back from shul in the darkness, my father asked if he could hold my hand so he wouldn't fall. It was then that I realized that as children, we never want to stop holding our parents' hands. And we never want to stop being their children. Nothing could be more meaningful to me than bringing *nachas* to my wonderful parents.

Rabbi and Mrs. Yehuda and Nusy Lefkovitz, my in-laws, have always treated me as a son. We treasure having them right in our neighborhood; their involvement in our lives enhances everything we do. They take great pride in my work and are a constant source of encouragement.

Mrs. Tova Salb seems to be an expert on whatever subject I am writing about. As my editor, she knows what I want to say and does her work with incredible efficiency and cheer. I do not know how she manages to edit everything so well, but I sure hope that she will continue to do so.

To the hundreds of people who have shared their stories with me: Thank you! Although I am not able to use each and every story, I am grateful nonetheless. I hope to make use of them in some way in the future. For various reasons, it is often necessary to camouflage the identity of the individuals involved in a story. In many instances in this book, I have taken the liberty of doing so, in order to protect the identity of the characters.

I would like to express my gratitude to the many institutions that have invited me to speak on their behalf. Thank you for keeping me in mind.

To my children, **Tzvi, Avromi, Efraim, Miri, Shmueli, Chana Leah, Henni,** and **Chayala:** Though at times I seem preoccupied with someone or something pertaining to my work, nothing in my life is more important than you.

And finally, to my wife, **Chumi** . . .

May the Al-mighty continue to bless us with immeasurable *siyata d'Shmaya*.

Yechiel Spero

Cheshvan 5775

INTRODUCTION

C*HIZUK.*

Encouragement. Strengthening.

Who doesn't need it? No matter who we are and what we do, *chizuk* is an essential part of our lives; it lifts us up and gives us hope. When we are down in the dumps and stuck in the doldrums, an encouraging word from another caring individual can give us the strength to conquer whatever stands in our way. Without it, well, who can bear the thought? We can't even continue to function.

Chizuk.

It is the oxygen of our emotional and spiritual existence. With it, we can overcome any obstacle that the evil inclination places in our path. Thus empowered, we have the confidence and strength to tackle even the most difficult *nisyonos* (tests).

There will be rainy days, days in which we don't even want to think about our *tzaros*, our painful situations, as individuals and as a nation. That is when *chizuk* is needed. It places us on pedestals, from where we can fend off even our worst enemies. It gives us a glimpse into who we can become. It is thrilling, invigorating, and allows us to dream of the impossible.

We must believe in ourselves; we must understand how great we can be. In order for that to happen, we need *chizuk*.

It is our light in the darkness, a lifeboat in the thrashing tidal wave of *galus*.

As the world continues to change, we are faced with more and more seemingly insurmountable tests. Having children. Raising children. *Shidduchim*. Livelihood. Health. It all seems so overwhelming.

We live in a world of many challenges and few solutions. No matter what our stage of life, we need encouragement.

In our youth, we face the seemingly insurmountable trials that the evil inclination places before us. The lures of secular society have such a strong magnetic pull that it is almost impossible not to stumble. For those times, we need *chizuk*.

As a person enters the stage of *shidduchim*, regardless of gender, it is hard to face rejection. And then, there are those who don't even receive a single suggestion or a phone call. This time of our lives can be filled with loneliness, and a person may sometimes grow despondent. As he or she continues to search for a soulmate, the single person may wonder if this stage will ever come to an end: "Will I ever find the right one?" For those times, we need *chizuk*.

Soon after we get married, we hope to be blessed with a child. But there are thousands among us who don't have such an easy time of it. The anxiety, worry, and sadness can crush them. As time goes on, the disappointment and loneliness only worsens, and many such couples cry themselves to sleep every night. For those times, we need *chizuk*.

So Hashem has blessed us with a family. Yet even with all the effort and *tefillos* we put into each child, there can still be challenges up ahead. Even when they come from the finest families, many of our youth are struggling to see the beauty and pleasure of a Torah life, to find themselves a place in society. Their parents may also be soaking their pillows each night, wondering where their children are — and how far they will stray. For those times, we need *chizuk*: for the parents and for the children.

Thousands of parents feel like they have failed because they can't afford to buy their children the clothes or gadgets that everyone else in the class takes for granted. The family car needs extensive repairs and the electric company is threatening to turn off the lights; the children are bored and listless during the summer months, since there is no money even for day camp. The head of the household has been laid off numerous times, and he wonders why he can't hold down a job like everyone else. For those times, we need *chizuk.*

Finally, as we grow older, our health becomes more frail and our bones more brittle. One begins to contemplate the shortness of life and worries that his spouse should be taken care of, come what may. He begins to wonder what he will say on his final day of reckoning. For those times, we need *chizuk.*

Yes, at every stage of our lives, we need encouragement to continue to fight and eventually persevere. This *chizuk* may come from the unlikeliest of sources. It may come from a stranger's encouraging word, or from an incident where we find that the *Ribbono Shel Olam* has sent us a "smile." Yes, we must look for *chizuk.* But when we do, we will find what we are looking for.

Even more important, we must look out for one another. We must take note of those around us who need help. They may not need money; they may just need a friend.

And anyone, regardless of who you are, can be a friend.

It was shortly after World War II, and Rav Yosef Shlomo Kahaneman, the Ponovezher Rav, was doing his utmost to rebuild the Jewish people and to restore the vast amounts of Torah study that had been lost. The newly reestablished Yeshivas Ponovezh in Bnei Brak was slowly beginning to gain a foothold and establish itself as one of the primary places of learning in Eretz Yisrael.

Financially, however, the yeshivah's situation was bleak. It was not unusual for Rav Kahaneman to have to borrow large sums of money to cover payroll, even if only for a day or two, until he was able to find some other way to cover his expenses.

One day, he called his trusted friend, Rav Yehoshua Zelig Diskin, the rav of Pardes Chana, and asked him for a favor. He had a very important meeting scheduled in Yerushalayim the following day, but he had arranged to borrow a large sum of money from someone in Bnei Brak. Since Rav Kahaneman would not be in Bnei Brak to pick up the money, he needed Rav Diskin to procure the loan for him.

Eager to help in any way possible, Rav Yehoshua Zelig happily secured the loan the next day and brought it over to the yeshivah, expecting to give the money to one of the rav's secretaries or assistants. As he entered the office, however, he was surprised to see the rav sitting in his office, with a small boy at his side. Wasn't he supposed to be at a meeting in Yerushalayim?

When the rav stood up to welcome Rav Yehoshua Zelig and thank him for his help, Rav Yehoshua Zelig noticed that the rav's eyes were red from crying. As Rav Yehoshua Zelig looked more carefully, he noticed that the little boy was crying, as well. Rav Kahaneman felt that Rav Yehoshua Zelig deserved an explanation.

"Whenever I leave Bnei Brak, I stop by the Batei Avos orphanage. When I came by today, I saw that this boy was crying. I bent down and asked him why he was crying, and he told me that he had just found out that his brother had died in the war.

"When he kept crying, I could not help but cry along with him."

He looked at his dear friend and asked with all sincerity, "How could I have left him alone at a time like this?"

Stories such as this one happen every day. You don't have to be the Ponovezher Rav to comfort a crying child, or a suffering adult. You just have to reach out and lend a hand, or a listening ear.

It is my hope that this book will provide encouragement and strength for those in need.

Because everyone needs. . .**A Touch of Chizuk.**

CONTENTS

NISYONOS

TEFILLAH

Emunah

Ahavas Yisrael

Limud Torah

CHINUCH

NECHAMAH

NISYONOS

A WELL-DESERVED PUNISHMENT

Years ago, when Chassidic courts abounded in Europe, whenever there was a wedding of the children or grandchildren of a great Rebbe, the Chassidim would travel from miles around to attend the memorable and festive event. The Chassidim basked in the spiritual aura of these celebrations, and they relished the opportunity to watch their Rebbe dance, enraptured in the moment.

WHEN A WEDDING TOOK PLACE BETWEEN THE grandchildren of the Rebbe of Husyatin and the Trisker Maggid, hundreds came from all over, each person eager to participate in his Rebbe's joy. But one Chassid, Herschel, had an ulterior motive, as well; he hoped to get a *berachah*.

Herschel's life was full of difficulties and challenges. Aside from his struggle to make a living, he had two children who were ill and two daughters who were having trouble with *shidduchim*. He was bitter about his situation in life and hoped to find some inspiration at this grand wedding.

The night of the wedding arrived and Herschel's Rebbe, the Husyatiner, was the first important personage to arrive. His Chassidim began singing and dancing at his behest. But after a short while, they began to wonder why his *mechutan*, the Trisker Maggid, had not yet put in an appearance. They perceived his late arrival as a show of disrespect to their leader. With each passing moment, the disciples became more and more agitated. Finally, after a wait of several hours, the Maggid arrived. His Chassidim ran to greet him, and they, too, began singing and dancing. At that point, preparations began in earnest for the *chuppah*.

Although some of the Chassidim had grown impatient, now that the wedding had begun, they forgot about their annoyance and were excited to participate in the *simchah*. But Herschel, with all of his bitterness, resented the fact that they had been kept waiting. Stewing inside, he decided that he was going to show the Trisker Maggid that his lateness was objectionable.

As the Maggid walked toward the *chuppah,* the sea of disciples before him split into two long rows, allowing him to walk through. As the Maggid passed, Herschel impulsively decided to do the unthinkable: he grabbed onto the Maggid's long flowing coat and tugged at it, preventing him from taking another step.

The Trisker Maggid felt the pull and stopped. At first, he thought that the coat had gotten caught on a nail, but when he turned around he saw a fellow holding onto his coat. As everyone turned to see what was happening, Herschel let go of the coat, now realizing what a foolish thing he had done. The Maggid looked at Herschel curiously but continued walking toward the *chuppah*.

When the *chuppah* was over, the attendees began discussing the episode. Shocked at this impudent behavior, they wondered what type of consequences Herschel would face. Word reached the Rebbe of Husyatin, who walked over to Herschel and motioned for him to go with the Rebbe to the Maggid.

"Trisker Maggid," the Rebbe said, "I know that you are not particular about your honor, but I insist that we take this man to a *din*

Torah. For if we do not deal with his unacceptable behavior down here on Earth, woe to him and to the punishment he may receive in Heaven."

The Maggid agreed to go with the Husyatiner Rebbe and Herschel to Rav Yekkele (Yaakov) Weidenfeld of Hermilov, author of *Kochav MiYaakov*. After listening to the Rebbe of Husyatin describe Herschel's impudent behavior, Rav Yekkele stated, "I don't believe that there is a clear-cut halachah regarding this in *Shulchan Aruch*. When this happens, we generally try to find a similar case and then we compare the two cases. As such, I want to tell you what happened in a similar situation, and from there I will be able to give my final decision."

And then he proceeded to tell the two Rebbes and Herschel the following story:

> *Many years ago, in the town of Ostraha, lived Moshe, a very generous and wise man, who was chosen as the rosh hakahal (head of the community), as he was admired and respected by all. In the same city, there lived a man named Aryeh, who struggled to support his family and suffered from numerous challenges.*
>
> *Aryeh was the one person in town who despised Moshe. He was so full of jealousy that he could not help himself. Every time he saw Moshe, he spewed forth vicious, hatred-filled curses. Moshe, an upstanding and forgiving man, tried his best to ignore the venomous verbal barbs. But even though he was willing to overlook the attacks, the rest of the community members were not. They were infuriated at the pauper's unacceptable and uncalled-for behavior. Finally, they decided to do something about the situation; they informed the Rebbe, Rav Yeibeh, of the insults being hurled at their beloved Moshe, and they demanded that the perpetrator be reprimanded and punished.*
>
> *Rav Yeibeh listened to the story and, after some thought,*

rendered his decision. "I feel that Reb Aryeh is attacking the kind and generous rosh hakahal for one reason: because he is suffering terribly. He is drowning in debt and overwhelmed with his personal trials and tribulations. However," and here he turned to Aryeh, "if you would see Reb Moshe's generosity up close, then you would feel the same way about him as everyone else. And so, I decree that Reb Moshe hire you to work for him. When you begin making ends meet and some of the financial pressure is lifted, you will feel indebted to him. The remorse you will then feel about your behavior will be the greatest punishment you could receive."

Then and there, Moshe hired Aryeh. In a relatively short period of time, Aryeh's fortunes changed. He was extremely grateful to the man he used to curse — and very ashamed at the way he had acted toward him.

Rav Yekkele finished recounting the story and turned toward Herschel. "You behaved in this manner only because you are so broken. You are suffering financially and you have a great deal of personal difficulty. However, if your situation were to improve, you would realize what a righteous individual the Maggid is. And so, I have decided that he will bless you that your fortunes will change. When you see that all of his blessings are fulfilled and your life begins to turn around, you will be so grateful to him that the shame you feel will atone for the sin you committed."

The Maggid smiled and blessed Herschel. Sure enough, in a few short months, his fortunes changed. Eventually, Herschel came to express his incredible gratitude and begged his newfound Rebbe for forgiveness.

Rav Dov Berish Weidenfeld, the Tchebiner Rav, who was Rav Yekkele's son, added the following thought. "When things don't go our way and our frustrations weigh us down, we tend to lash out at HaKadosh Baruch Hu. But if our struggles were to disappear and our situation were to improve, we would see up close how kind and generous and giving He is. And so, we ask the Al-mighty to bless us and take away our suffering and pain; once this happens, we will be able to witness His kindness and benevolence. When we do, we will be filled with remorse and shame, and truly regret that we treated Him in such an unseemly manner. This will help us atone for our sins and give us the closeness for which we yearn."

TEN MINUTES
OF ETERNITY

O NE YEAR HAD PASSED SINCE THE TRAGIC PASSING OF Chaim'ke Tivoni, a simple and beloved carpenter. The loss took its toll on the widow and four orphans he left behind. During *shivah,* people told over stories of Chaim'ke's generosity and kindness, how he often told his customers to pay him later — and later never came. Additionally, aside from rickety tables, unbalanced chests, broken cabinets, and bookcases, Chaim'ke fixed many broken hearts. His ever-cheerful demeanor and simple but ironclad approach to *emunah* gave needy individuals much encouragement and hope, even as they coped with their difficulties. Indeed, Chaim'ke was very beloved and dear to those who had known him.

Still, no matter how many people came with words of comfort during the days of *shivah*, no real solace could be found. While the words enhanced the family's impression of their husband and father, they did not help pay the many bills and debts that had accrued. People mistakenly assumed that the family members were not in need of financial assistance, and no one offered to help them pay off their overwhelming debts.

Orna, his wife, did her utmost to hold it together. She took on extra jobs but found herself drowning in debt and frustration. When Chaim'ke was alive, he infused in her and the children the unquestionable truth that Hashem is always and will always be helping them. But with her husband no longer there to provide material and emotional support, she was floundering and losing hope.

Now, at the end of this difficult year, Orna went to the cemetery with her children, where they davened a lot and cried even more. She always tried to be strong for her children and to put on a good face, but standing there at his grave, she could no longer hold back her tears. The difficulties she had endured during the year since Chaim'ke's death — both emotional and financial — now overwhelmed her. After the children finished reciting their specifically chosen chapters of *Tehilim*, she asked them if she could have a few private moments to daven. They stepped back and allowed their mother her privacy.

As soon as they were no longer within earshot, she directed her voice toward his *kever*. In a tear-choked voice she said, "Chaim'ke, I know that you were a very kind and caring person and that you fulfilled your task on This Earth. And I also understand that it was decreed that I should be a widow and that my children should be orphans. But it is so difficult for me to do it all without you. I am asking you to please be a *meilitz yosher* (advocate) for our family, that things should get easier."

As Orna spoke, the tears flowed freely onto her husband's *matzeivah*. Suddenly, she heard a voice behind her. When she turned around, she saw an elderly man, tall and handsome, with a trimmed beard. He had driven up in a limousine and seemed to be searching for a grave. Finally, he made his way over to where she was standing.

He looked at the grave, then at Orna, and asked, "Are you Chaim'ke's widow?"

She acknowledged that she was and then she asked him for his name. "My name is Yosef."

As Orna and her children began to converse with Yosef, he pulled a *yahrtzeit licht* from his pocket and placed it upon Chaim's tombstone. Orna asked the man, "Did you know my husband?"

"Yes and no," he replied ambiguously. "Well, I knew him for only about 10 minutes." The children looked at their mother in confusion, and then they all looked back at the tall, prestigious-looking stranger, as they waited for an explanation. It was not long in coming.

A year ago, I, too, was a patient in the oncology department of the hospital. Along with the chemotherapy treatments, the doctors recommended surgery. Before the surgery, I took a walk around the hospital. As I passed the hospital shul, I said to myself, "Yosef, you are almost 80 years old and you have no idea how long you're going to live. You have not been inside a synagogue in 67 years, since the day you became a bar mitzvah. If there was ever a time that you needed to pray, it is now."

As I walked into the room, I could see that the sun was setting. Out of the corner of my eye, I noticed a man. His head was inside the aron kodesh, and I could hear him crying. I didn't want to disturb him so I stood there quietly as I listened to what he was saying. His prayer would change my life.

He cried, "Dear Father, I love You so much, and I thank You for everything that You've given me. I thank You for a wonderful wife and four beautiful children. I thank You for my house and I thank You for my job. I thank You for all the wonderful years I've lived. And dear Father, I also thank You for this illness. Most people look at an illness as a curse, but I see it as a blessing in disguise. I know that the words machalah [illness] and mechilah [forgiveness] are closely related because when one has a sickness, it brings him forgiveness for all of his wrongdoings. It is difficult for me to breathe and my body is racked with pain. And I thank You for all of that.

"I am nothing more than a simple carpenter, but for these past two years that I have endured the treatments and the pain, my soul has been elevated to the foot of Your Heavenly Throne. I know the value of every blessing I make and every prayer I say. I cherish every moment I have to learn, and I no longer value the silliness and the desires of This World. All I want is to be in Your hands.

"Dear Father, I am most probably going to be on This Earth for no more than another week or so, and then I will be with You. Please, when I come up to You, hold me and kiss me as Your son. I have no other desire than to love You and be with You.

"For I am Your son who awaits Your love, Chaim'ke."

Yosef recounted the entire episode as if it had happened that very day. "Even after he finished his magnificent speech," Yosef continued, "Chaim'ke did not know or notice that I was there. He left the room, went to the elevator, and pressed the button to go to the third floor. My room was also on the third floor, and I was amazed to discover that I was in the room next to his. We were neighbors. I wanted to speak to him but I couldn't build up the courage. Finally, after a few days, I walked over to the nurse and asked her how he was doing. But she was silent. Chaim'ke was gone."

At this point, he directed his comments to Chaim'ke's wife and children. "It is because of your husband and father that I remember the Father I had long ago forgotten. I could have died like an animal without knowing that there was Someone Who loves me, Who is waiting to hold me. I could have died without doing any more mitzvos. I know that I don't have a long time to live, but for the bit that I do have, I want to live as a true Torah Jew. And the merit for that goes to Chaim'ke."

They were stunned by his words. There was a long silence, and then he thanked them and slowly walked away.

One year passed.

It was once again the day of Chaim'ke's *yahrtzeit*. His wife and children were about to head out to the cemetery, when Orna received a letter in the mail, with a return address that she did not recognize: the law offices of Tziyon Ben Harush. She opened the envelope and saw that there were 10 pages stapled together, with a note attached:

"Geveret Tivoni, this is a copy of the will of Yosef Herblit. There's no reason for you to read the entire document. Only Number 17 pertains to you."

She quickly looked for Number 17. When she read what it said, she nearly fainted. Yosef had instructed his lawyers to give $400,000 to Mordechai, Reuven, Yaakov, and Shimon, the children of Chaim and Orna Tivoni. Beneath the instructions was the number of the account in Bank Leumi in Tel Aviv. Each child would receive $100,000.

On the back page, there was a copy of a note, written in Yosef's handwriting.

"Geveret Tivoni, it is only because of your husband that I will be fortunate enough to receive a place to live, a *home*, in the Next World. Therefore, I feel an obligation to be a partner in helping to build a *home* for your children in This World. It is impossible to measure the amount of gratitude and appreciation I feel toward your husband, whom I was not privileged to know for more than 10 minutes. But those 10 minutes changed my life until the end of time.

"With much blessing, Yosef Herblit."

Orna stared at the paper in disbelief. Tears streamed down her cheeks. There were no words to express her feelings at the moment. But as she turned her eyes toward Heaven, she managed two:

"Thank You."

Rav Shlomo Wolbe explains that when a loved one is niftar, the deceased is not gone; rather, he or she is living on a faraway island, where he cannot communicate with his loved ones. But his loved ones, who are still in This World, are able to communicate with him. In addition, even though the individual has left This World, he can advocate on their behalf, as a meilitz yosher.

What a comforting thought for someone who has lost a loved one.

But there is another lesson to be learned from this incredible story. We encounter thousands of people in our lives, and most of those encounters seem incidental. But each one of those "chance meetings" can affect the people we meet in an eternal way.

What an inspiring thought. What an awesome responsibility.

KING OF THE MOUNTAIN

In 1967, the Jewish world witnessed countless miracles as the Israeli Army — outnumbered in terms of troops and facing a 4-to-1 disadvantage in terms of artillery — vanquished four armies and tripled the size of its land. Seeing firsthand the undeniable fingerprints of the Ribbono Shel Olam, thousands of people returned to their roots and many people became baalei teshuvah. This unprecedented response carried great momentum.

Rav Shlomo Wolbe wrote numerous essays describing the historical change in the landscape of Jewish thought and emotion engendered by this victory. This collection, titled Bein Sheishess LeAsor, was later renamed Olam HaYedidus.

I N THE *SEFER*, RAV WOLBE RECOUNTS HOW HE ONCE FOUND himself hunkered down with many of his *talmidim* from Yeshivas Be'er Yaakov in a *miklat* (shelter). The young men were scared. There had been a relative calm for the 10 years preceding this war, and this was the boys' first exposure to the fear and apprehension associated with war.

With the Jewish people in imminent danger, Rav Wolbe spoke to his *talmidim* on the topic of *emunah*. He said that there are no atheists in foxholes; everyone believes during times of war. Yes, there may be professors who discuss the possibility of G-d's existence while lecturing in a classroom, but when people are facing the enemy, and guns and bombs are exploding all around them, everyone believes in the Al-mighty.

The young men listened intently and absorbed the words of their rebbi. They all considered themselves believers; they didn't need the fear of war to convince them that there is a *Ribbono Shel Olam*. But to punctuate this point, Rav Wolbe told them the story of an Israeli ship that was being targeted by Egyptian gunfire. On the ship was a group of young *kibbutzniks* from HaShomer HaTzair, a socialist Zionist youth group completely unaffiliated with Torah and outspoken in its defiance of Hashem. While they were being targeted, the *kibbutzniks* stood on deck and screamed, "*Shema Yisrael Hashem Elokeinu Hashem Echad.*"

One of the young men in the bunker listened to the story and then asked Rav Wolbe, "Rebbi, I understand that it is admirable and perhaps even remarkable that these *kibbutzniks* showed such great faith and expressed their true feelings of *emunah* when they were pushed up against the wall. But what happened the next morning? Did these people don *tefillin*? Did they change?"

Rav Wolbe contemplated the question and thought carefully

before responding. "If you don't mind, let me ask you a question. A few months ago, you, along with the rest of us, stood in shul at the end of *Ne'ilah*. With your life hanging in the balance, you screamed from the depths of your heart, '*Shema Yisrael Hashem Elokeinu Hashem Echad.*' Tell me, the next morning, when you walked into shul to put on *tefillin*, was it a life-altering experience for you? Were you so much different from the day before?"

The young man could not help but smile, as he understood his rebbi's point.

Rav Wolbe continued, "To answer your question, I don't know if they put on *tefillin* the next day. It is difficult to respond to the question in *Tehillim* [24:3]: '*Mi yaaleh ve'har Hashem* — Who may ascend the mountain of Hashem?' However, it is even more difficult to answer the call of '*U'mi yakum bimkom kadsho* — And who may stand in the place of His sanctity?'"

Indeed, it is difficult to ascend the mountain in the first place. However, to stay there may be even harder. It takes work, effort, and renewed commitment each and every day. No, it is not easy at all.

When I heard this magnificent thought, a childhood memory came to mind. Growing up in Cleveland, huge snowstorms were not unusual. When the plows were finished pushing away the snow, there would be tall mountains at the edge of our driveways and in the backyard of the Hebrew Academy, where I went to school.

One of our favorite pastimes at those times was playing "King of the Mountain." The object of the game was simple. The person who was "king" had to climb to the top of the mountain. Once he got there, he had to fend off anyone who tried to knock him off the mountain. It was difficult to reach the top of the mountain. But once you got there, it was an incredible feeling. If I recall correctly, we never stayed there for long. Usually, within a few moments, someone else became "king." But we knew that once we ascended the mountain, even if we were knocked off, we could get back there.

> *In light of Rav Wolbe's beautiful lesson, which was taught in a dark, war-torn miklat, I would humbly suggest that reaching the apex of the spiritual mountain is a daunting task. True, it is much more difficult to remain there. But if you set your mind to it and reach the peak, you will always know that even if something or someone knocks you off, you always have the strength, wherewithal, and perseverance to reach the top again. Because you have been there before.*

THE MIDDLE OF THE STORY

ON THE FOURTH OF SHEVAT, 5744, NEARLY 100,000 PEOple flooded the streets of Netivot as they headed toward the funeral of the Baba Sali, Rav Yisrael Abuchatzeira, the great *mekubal* and holy adviser. On the way to the funeral, a car carrying four men was involved in a fatal collision, leaving behind four widows and over 30 orphans.

Rav Erlanger, a *mashpia* (spiritual adviser) in Eretz Yisrael, tried to find the proper words to express the message that should be taken from this tragedy. Eager to seek guidance, he turned to the Rachmastrivka Rebbe and asked him, "What can be done at a time like this?" But the Rebbe shrugged his shoulders; he had no answer for Rav Erlanger. Rav Erlanger asked again, with more persistence. "What can we do at a time of such difficulty?"

The Rebbe looked at him and responded emphatically, "What can be done? Everything can be done!" Rav Erlanger appreciated the Rebbe's bluntness.

If the Al-mighty did not reveal His reasons, it is not our job to try to figure them out. Instead, when tragedy strikes, we should focus our efforts on improving — in any way we can.

There is a well-known Yalkut Shimoni (Yeshayah 393) that states that the world will last for 6,000 years and then will cease to exist as we know it.

Someone once asked Rav Mottel of Slonim, "What will you do if the world continues to exist as we know it even after 6,000 years?" He answered, "I will wake up in the morning, take my *tallis* and *tefillin*, go to the *beis midrash* and daven, just as I always have. And I will conclude that I misunderstood that particular statement from Chazal.

"Just because I misunderstood it, it doesn't mean that it is not true, and that is the basis of all *emunah*. I must continue to do that which the Al-mighty demands. Without questions. And perhaps without fully understanding. We don't have to know; we have to believe."

Three times a day, we say in the tefillah of Ashrei (Tehillim 145:20), "Shomer Hashem es kol ohavav, ve'eis kol ha'reshaim yashmid — Hashem protects all who love Him, and all the wicked He will destroy."

A well-meaning but unlearned Jew entered a shul, as the *chazzan* was reciting the first part of the above verse, but he did not hear the end. Thus, all he picked up was: "*Shomer Hashem es kol ohavav, ve'eis kol ha'reshaim* — Hashem protects all who love Him, and all the wicked." The fellow was perplexed. He could readily understand that Hashem watches over His beloved *tzaddikim*; their righteousness and piety earn them that privilege. But why would He guard the wicked? The man assumed that this highlighted the limitless compassion of Hashem for all of His creatures, even the wicked.

The next day, the simpleminded Jew walked into the shul, and caught only the end of the *pasuk,* once again out of context: "*Es kol ohavav ve'eis kol ha'reshaim yashmid* — All who love Him, and all the wicked, He will destroy." Once more, he was bewildered. How could the Al-mighty destroy the righteous along with the wicked?

Searching for answers, the simpleton approached his rabbi. The rabbi answered the foolish question with a short and sharp response: "You came in the middle."

> This retort is the answer to all our questions. When we look around and see that there are wicked people who are enjoying themselves, we suppose that it is because the Al-mighty is merciful even to those who are wicked. But when we see the righteous suffering, we can no longer comprehend His ways.
>
> We must realize that we came in the middle of a long and complex existence. Hashem's infinite calculations and wisdom preceded ours by thousands of years. We are only looking at a small snippet of time. Trying to decipher the cryptic codes of Creation is both foolish and naïve.
>
> Therefore, when we hear of unspeakable tragedies that rattle our senses, we must learn to accept. And move on.
>
> Because you can't ask questions on the plot when you arrive in the middle of the story.

A Beautiful
Bas Mitzvah Gift

B ATYA GREW UP IN RUSSIA UNDER THE COMMUNIST regime, certainly not the ideal setting in which a Jewish girl could strengthen her commitment to Torah Judaism.

To celebrate her bas mitzvah, a *Kiddush* was planned in Batya's honor, and her mother prepared a special *kugel* for the men of the community. At the *Kiddush,* Batya's father spoke about the importance of following in the footsteps of our ancestors. He pleaded with his daughter to adhere to the precepts of Torah and *Yiddishkeit*. Then he asked those who were present to please give his daughter a gift.

They looked at him in surprise. They barely had food to eat, and he was asking for a present? Then he clarified his request. "I am not asking for money or for books. I am asking for a present that will last my daughter a lifetime. If you can take a few moments and share with my Batya a story from your life, one in which you encountered difficulty and challenge and were able to overcome, that will make a meaningful gift."

Each person stood up and shared a personal vignette. Every individual's challenge was a different one, but they all imparted how they were able to confront those tribulations. Finally, it was the last gentleman's turn.

Reb Dovid was very well respected in the village. He had some physical challenges, a visible limp just to name the most obvious one. However, with a bit of assistance, he stood up and addressed the crowd.

> *When I was young, I learned in yeshivah. I was blessed with a very good head and I was very successful. However, the many*

*forces of spiritual danger that abounded threatened to uproot
everything I had learned. My parents and my teachers warned
me about the dangers. Yet wherever I turned, individuals were
waiting to introduce me to material that was detrimental to
my spiritual health and well-being. I began to read the news-
papers and went to the social gatherings in the libraries. One
thing led to another. Before long, I left yeshivah altogether.*

*I channeled all my efforts into improving my language
skills, and I became a master linguist, excelling at the use of
words. In particular, my talent for poetry gained acclaim. People who read my writings encouraged me to pursue a career
as a writer and assured me that I would achieve international
fame as a poet. They promised that my name would be syn-
onymous with the great poets of history.*

*But then one day, everything changed. I was stepping into
the street when a car came whizzing by. I didn't have a chance
to move out of the way, and it ran me over. I was severely
injured; my feet were crushed and my spirit was broken. I
went through many operations, as the doctors tried repeatedly
to repair my damaged leg. Eventually, they had no choice but
to amputate my leg and replace it with a wooden one.*

Every set of eyes in the room was glued to Reb Dovid as he
relayed his riveting account. When he mentioned the detail about
an artificial leg, there was an audible gasp from the people at the
Kiddush. Apparently, although everyone knew that he limped, very
few had ever heard the story about how he developed the limp and
didn't know that he had an artificial leg. Reb Dovid continued his
account:

*I was broken beyond measure. I walked around depressed and
miserable. One day, I met my old mashgiach from yeshivah. He
asked me how I was doing and I broke down crying. He didn't
give me the "I told you so" routine. Rather, he tried to encourage me and lift me up. Finally, he said to me, "I know you feel*

like your life is over. You feel like you're broken. But why not use that which remains?"

At first, I had no idea what he was talking about. Soon enough, he clarified. "Your body may be broken, yet your mind is as fresh and sharp and creative as ever. Why not continue learning? No one is judging you. No one will look at you differently. You are a brilliant fellow. Formulate original chiddushim [novel Torah thoughts]; share your chaburos [discourses] with the others in the beis midrash. They will marvel at your wondrous words of wisdom and Torah. And you will develop a sense of sipuk hanefesh [fulfillment] and satisfaction from it all."

I listened to his lifesaving words. I decided right then and there that I was going to go back to learning. Within a few years, I was blessed with a wonderful wife, who looked past my leg and saw someone who was thirsty for Torah learning. She admired me for who I really was. And from that day forward, I continued to learn. We built a beautiful life together and have a wonderful family, all of us following in the footsteps of our age-old traditions.

Reb Dovid finished his story and then spoke with great emotion. "Batya, the greatest gift I ever received was the accident that destroyed my leg. It was only because of my accident that today I have the life that I do, with the family that I have. Without that accident, I would have been nothing more than a drunkard and a miserable, depressed human being.

"Batya, take my message to heart. All of the accidents, challenges, and difficulties that you face throughout your lifetime are only concealed gifts from Hashem, to lift you higher and higher, so you can achieve your true purpose in life. If you listen to me, your life will be enriched forever."

Batya took these words to heart. She has endured many "accidents" during her lifetime, and has allowed each one to enrich her life further and further.

LIMITED TIME

Rav Chaim Friedlander, a disciple of Rav Eliyahu Eliezer Dessler, was the mashgiach in Yeshivas Ponovezh in Bnei Brak. His sefarim on the tefillos of the Yamim Noraim as well as on hashkafas hachaim (life philosophy) have been met with great acceptance and praise.

When I was engaged, his pamphlet titled "Ve'yadata Ki Shalom Ohalecha," a guide for chasanim, made a great impact on me. While his sefarim on hashkafah plumb the depths of the Ramchal and lend meaning to esoteric concepts, this small booklet is down to earth and practical. It teaches young men about the basic principles of marriage, and how to be sensitive to their wives.

While I have always treasured this sefer, a story that I heard recently put it into an entirely new light. This story helped me realize that we can never stop working on improving ourselves. Rav Chaim's never-ending quest to refine his character exemplifies how one must approach life — whether in marriage or in any other endeavor.

RAV CHAIM WAS IN HIS EARLY 60'S WHEN HE BEGAN TO feel throbbing pain in his mouth. He went from doctor to doctor, until one decided to do some extensive testing. The results were disturbing; there was a tumor in his mouth that required immediate attention.

Rav Chaim traveled to the best hospitals in America in search of a cure. After administering treatment for a number of weeks, the doctors were satisfied with his progress. He returned to Eretz Yisrael, where he continued his rigorous schedule of delivering *shmuessen* (discourses), both in Ponovezh and in Yeshivat HaNe-gev, as well as *vaadim* and *chaburos* (different types of group dis-cussions).

When he was too weak to leave his home, *avreichim* (*kollel* fellows) came to his house to glean from his wisdom. Although he was still a very sick man, he did not publicize his illness; he refused to slow down or curtail his schedule. Those who knew of his condition were startled at his strength and perseverance.

Unfortunately, his illness continued to spread. As the tumors grew, he became weaker and weaker. He consulted with his doc-tor, who made it clear that his time on This Earth was limited. The doctor agreed to continue to see him and treat him, but the main purpose was just to make him comfortable and limit his pain.

From the doctor's office, Rav Chaim went straight to the home of his rebbi, Rav Shach, to discuss his situation and seek his advice. Knowing that his rebbi's door was always open, he stepped into his apartment. He was surprised to see that the door to the room where Rav Shach learned was closed, for there was a meeting of the yeshivah administration going on at the moment. Rav Chaim waited outside the room.

Soon, a young man entered the waiting room and explained to Rav Chaim that he had also come to seek Rav Shach's advice. The young fellow recognized Rav Chaim and knew that he was a member of the administration. He realized that Rav Chaim had not joined the meeting out of humility; Rav Chaim did not want to dis-turb the meeting after it had started. The *bachur* took the liberty of opening the door so Rav Chaim could enter and join the meeting.

As soon as he entered the room, everyone present stood up, to accord him the proper honor. A frail shell of his former self, the mere sight of him brought tears to their eyes. His condition had deteriorated so much over the past few weeks that he didn't even have the strength to close the door behind him.

After a few minutes, he was finally able to work his way up to the front of the room, where Rav Shach was seated. He leaned over and whispered something to Rav Shach, who asked Rav Chaim a number of questions. For each question, Rav Chaim gave a short reply.

After a few moments, Rav Chaim turned to leave. The young man who had observed the entire scene had no idea what had happened. The only thing he knew was that everyone in the room was crying.

Later that day, the *bachur's* curiosity got the better of him. He approached one of the rebbeim in the yeshivah and said, "I saw that everyone in the room was crying. If this is something that I should not know about and should not be asking, I will walk away. But if there's something that can be shared, I would really like to know."

The rebbi thought for a moment or two and then responded, "I will tell you on one condition. You cannot tell anyone anything about this for the next month." After receiving the boy's consent, the rebbi told him what had occurred in the room:

Rav Chaim walked up to Rav Shach, and he told him that he had just come back from a doctor's appointment. The doctor had informed him that since there was nothing to do to cure him, he would just be giving him morphine to take away his pain.

When Rav Chaim had asked the doctor how much longer he has to live, the doctor told him that he has no more than two to three weeks. That is why he went immediately to Rav Shach, and that is why everyone in the room was crying.

However, he didn't come just to tell the rosh yeshivah that his time was limited. He came to find out: What should he work on in the last weeks of his life? Should he make a cheshbon hanefesh (introspection)? Should he do teshuvah? Should he spend his time reviewing everything that he had learned, so that he can come up to Shamayim with a freshness and clarity in his learning? Should he finish the sefer he was working on?

Should he set aside time to be with his children?

Rav Shach told him that when someone has a limited time left in this world, he should spend that time working on improving his middos.

Upon hearing the response, Rav Chaim thanked Rav Shach and left the room.

He had work to do.
His time was limited.

ALL TYPES OF YARMULKES

Rav Gamliel Rabinovitch told two stories of a special individual and the manner in which he conducted himself.

R AV AVROHOM, A RESPECTED AND PROMINENT RAV, WAS asked to conduct the marriage ceremony at the wedding of one of his congregants. When he arrived at the wedding hall, he noticed that the groom had a number of relatives who were not religious.

He walked toward the table where the *chassan* was sitting and reciting *Tehillim,* as the orchestra played soft and soul-stirring music. The young man, a sincere *bachur,* understood the significance of the moment. When his guests walked in and wished him mazel tov, he smiled and thanked them for coming. Then he returned to his *Tehillim* and continued reciting his prayers.

His nonreligious relatives were amazed at the contrast between the lightheadedness and gaiety that marked their weddings, and the feeling of holiness that pervaded this *simchah*. Still, they did not feel that the pre-ceremony seriousness compromised the joy of the wedding.

A group of the relatives decided to approach the rabbi and introduce themselves. By that time, the room was filled with wedding guests. As each man was about to greet the rabbi, he reached into his pocket, pulled out a yarmulke, and placed it on his head. Only one fellow was so removed from religion that he didn't even own a head covering for such occasions.

When they reached Rav Avrohom, the rav stood up and gave them his full attention. He greeted each one warmly and smiled cheerfully. They were grateful to have the opportunity to shake the rabbi's hand and receive a blessing. Each person had his moment of connection with the rabbi, and walked away with newfound respect.

The man without the spare yarmulke tried to find someone who could lend him one, but no one could accommodate him. And then, his turn came. He stood in front of the rabbi, red faced and embarrassed; he knew that speaking to a rabbi without a yarmulke is disrespectful. As he shook the rabbi's hand, he apologized profusely for not wearing a *kippah,* and explained that he had tried to borrow one but nobody had a spare. So he tried his luck with the rabbi: "*Kvod harav*, would you happen to have a spare *kippah* for me?" He assumed that one of the rabbi's jobs was to carry extra skullcaps in his pocket.

The rabbi began to explain that he did not carry spare yarmulkes, but stopped himself. He reached under his hat and pulled out his own large yarmulke. He placed it gently on the man's head and assured him that since he himself was wearing a hat, he didn't need the yarmulke. In fact, he told the man that he could keep it.

The secular fellow was overwhelmed with emotion at the rav's selfless gesture, and tears began to form in his eyes. He held the yarmulke and rubbed his hands over the smooth velvet. In a burst of inspiration, he put both hands around the rabbi's hands and promised that he would never take the yarmulke off — for the rest of his life.

In the next story, the sensitive rav took his kindness and self-lessness one step further.

The prisons in Israel are filled with hardened criminals, some of whom have committed the worst crimes. Still, it is never too late to repent. Rabbis are encouraged to speak to the inmates, to lift their spirits, and try to get them to improve their ways.

Many of the inmates barely know anything about their religion. Nevertheless, whenever a rabbi comes, they do their utmost to show him the proper respect and honor. To that end, when they go to the rabbi's classes, they make sure to put on a yarmulke.

Rav Avrohom's lectures were popular among the inmates. His words of inspiration were like a beacon of light in their world of darkness. Before one class, a large crowd gathered. When the rav entered the room, the prisoners placed their *kippot* on their heads. Everyone except for one person.

Uri, a muscular fellow, looked around the room and realized that everyone had a head covering except for him. He was extremely embarrassed. To make matters worse, the other inmates took note and teased him. Some even chided him for his lack of respect for rabbis.

Although the rav had taken off his yarmulke from under his hat in the previous story, this time it was not so simple. One of the rules in the prison is that all visitors must check in their hats as they go through security. As such, Rav Avrohom couldn't offer Uri his yarmulke.

Or could he?

Rav Avrohom saw how disappointed Uri was with himself. His compassion aroused, he removed a handkerchief from his pocket and handed the prisoner his own yarmulke. Hence, the prisoner wore a beautiful black velvet yarmulke, while the rabbi had a white handkerchief tied around his head.

The prisoner uttered the same response that the rabbi had heard at his congregant's wedding: "Thank you so much for doing this for me. I will not take this kindness lightly. I will never take off this *kippah* for the rest of my life."

These two stories reminded me of a third story, one which I was privileged to hear firsthand.

The Talmudical Academy of Baltimore was privileged to host the famous Russian *refusenik*, Rabbi Yosef Mendelevich. He gave a riveting speech about his experiences in Communist Russia, where he fought fiercely for the freedom to practice his religion. He even tried to hijack a plane and take it to Israel. However, he was set up and the KGB threw him into prison. While serving time in the Russian Gulag, he learned to daven and keep mitzvos.

The prison guards did everything they could to break his spirit. To offset their abuse, he would go on extended hunger strikes. He wanted to show them that his commitment was greater than theirs; he was willing to fight for his freedom more than they were willing to fight to take it away from him.

Perhaps the vignette that inspired me most was the story of his head covering. While in prison, Yosef did not wear a traditional yarmulke. Rather, he took a handkerchief and wrapped it around his head, and that served as his *kippah*. As he spoke to us, he took out a similar-looking handkerchief and tied it around his head, just like he had so many years before. Although it was a constant battle, he managed to wear his head covering all the time.

One day, his father came to visit him. This was a rare occurrence, as his father was not well and it was difficult for him to make the long journey to the Gulag. Once again, the guards decided to test Yosef's will. Before he was allowed to leave his cell and greet his father who was waiting in the waiting room, he was told that he had to remove his head covering.

Yosef was faced with a dreadful dilemma. He knew that he was permitted by Jewish law to remove his head covering. However, he also knew that if he gives in now, then they will have broken his spirit — and defeated him. And so, he refused to take it off, but the prison authorities would not budge either. In this epic battle of wills, the heartless guards would not give in and they refused to allow him to see his father. Thus, instead of going through the door and running into his father's arms and hugging him and kissing him, Yosef remained in his miserable, lonely cell.

Tragically, he would never see his father again; he died a short while later.

Reb Yosef told this story before a packed audience of teenage boys, wearing the handkerchief on his head, just as he had in the Russian Gulag.

The boys were mesmerized. They could not imagine that the individual before them had passed such a difficult test. This was the stuff of legends.

After the speech was over, one of my students told me that while playing basketball, as he is running toward the basket, his yarmulke sometimes falls off. He knows that he should stop and pick it up, but it's in the middle of the game and it's too much of a sacrifice.

But after hearing a story like this, he can't help but wonder: Is it really such a sacrifice?

THE SEAMSTRESS'S SCISSORS

BINYAMIN ROTHMAN, A FEISTY AND ENERGETIC 3-YEAR-old, made sure to keep himself busy. This was not the type of child who sat quietly and colored in a coloring book. If it was quiet in the house for more than a few moments, his parents would grow concerned, for this was a sure sign that there was some mischief brewing.

One day, Mrs. Rothman was cooking in the kitchen when she noticed that it had been quiet for some time. When she stepped outside to check on Binyamin, she was horrified to discover that her son was hanging in midair, with a rope around his neck! She ran over to take him down, and saw that his face was blue; his oxygen supply must have been cut off a few minutes before. She screamed at the top of her lungs for help. Within minutes, an ambulance arrived and took Binyamin and his mother to the local hospital.

The moment the ambulance screamed its way into the hospital emergency room, a group of doctors and nurses surrounded the child. They whisked him into a room, where they worked on him feverishly. Mrs. Rothman stood on the side and prayed fervently for her son's recovery. With his life hanging in the balance, she whispered any words of *Tehilim* that came to her mind.

Though she tried her best to concentrate on the words she was saying, various thoughts raced through her mind, as feelings of guilt engulfed her. Why hadn't she watched him more carefully? Why did she just assume that he would be safe outside?

After a short while, the doctor came over to her. Her husband had just arrived, so the doctor sat down next to them to explain their son's condition. "He will live." Just as they began to breathe a sigh of relief, the doctor continued with further news that would dampen their spirits. "Yet there may be some significant damage to his brain, because he was without oxygen for a few minutes. He is now unconscious, and the next 24 hours are crucial."

Rabbi and Mrs. Rothman badgered him with questions, but the doctor didn't really have any answers. "For now, that is all the information I can give you."

After 24 hours, there was still no change. The doctors tried to reassure them and comfort them, but as the days turned into weeks, Binyamin's prognosis seemed bleaker and bleaker. It appeared that all hope was slipping away.

Rabbi and Mrs. Rothman took turns in the hospital during the day, but at night they slept at home. They realized that they would have to get their sleep in order to face the difficult challenges that lay ahead.

One morning, the phone rang at 6:10. Rabbi Rothman answered immediately. Although he never slept for many hours consecutively, his state of constant exhaustion caused him to maximize the sleep he was able to grab. Even so, he had trained himself to be fully awake within a moment.

"This is Dovid Frankel speaking," said the voice on the other end.

Reb Dovid was a confidant of the Chazon Ish. Additionally, he was a cousin of theirs. Still, his call at this hour was completely unexpected.

Dovid spoke with a sense of urgency in his voice. "Listen, I had a dream last night, and it is connected to you." Then he told Rabbi Rothman his dream:

> *I saw the Heavenly Court. In front of them there was a table, and on that table there were three boxes. On the right-hand side was a box labeled Life, and on the left-hand side there was a box labeled Death. In the middle, there was a box filled with pieces of paper with names on them.*

I watched as one of the angels picked up a piece of paper from the middle box. There was some discussion as to whether the paper should be placed in the Death box or the Life box. After a number of names were pulled out, each name accompanied by a discussion, the name of your son was announced.

Suddenly, I found myself in a fabric store in the middle of the Machaneh Yehudah Shuk. On the table in front of me, I saw a pair of blue scissors. The next thing I knew, the blue scissors were cutting up the paper with your son's name on it.

And then, I woke up.

"I don't know the meaning of the dream," concluded Reb Dovid. "However, I am certain that you will have a better idea of what it means."

Reb Dovid blessed Rabbi Rothman that Binyamin should have a *refuah sheleimah* (full recovery) and hung up the phone. It was now 6:15.

Once more, the phone rang. This time, it was the hospital. The person on the phone was calling with an urgent message: "We need you to come down to the hospital immediately. We are unable to give you any information over the phone."

Just like that, the phone call was over. Rabbi Rothman was beside himself. What could the hospital personnel want? Why didn't they tell him over the phone? He was sure it was bad news. Rabbi and Mrs. Rothman went as quickly as they could to the hospital. As they ran into Binyamin's room, they grew alarmed when they saw that he was not in his bed. Then they saw the doctor standing there, and their hearts dropped and they braced for the worst.

The doctor looked like he was in shock as he said, "We have no explanation for what happened. The morning began as all other mornings, and we were doing our normal rounds. Then, out of nowhere, your son woke up. He didn't just wake up, though; he snapped out of it completely. It was as if nothing had ever happened. The only description for this is: medical miracle. He is not in the room now because we could no longer keep him here; he is off and running somewhere!"

The doctor concluded by telling them something they already knew: "It is a miracle! You have much to be grateful for."

After Binyamin underwent further testing, the Rothmans packed his belongings and brought him home. On the way home, Rabbi Rothman remembered the phone call he had received earlier from their cousin Reb Dovid Frankel, which he had not had time to discuss with his wife. Now, finally, he told her the dream. As he spoke, he tried to find some interpretation but he came up blank. However, when he turned to his wife, he saw that her face was white and she was shaking.

She calmed down a bit and then explained, "The blue scissors he saw in the dream are my scissors. In my part-time work as a seamstress, I go to the textile store in Machaneh Yehudah to purchase different types of fabrics. Although they measure the fabrics for me, I always bring along my own scissors so that the cut is a bit cleaner and more precise.

"Yesterday, I went to purchase some material. Generally, I hand the man my scissors. However, as a special *zechus* [merit] for Binyamin, I decided to put up an extra fence in the area of *tzniyus* [modesty]. Therefore, instead of handing the scissors directly into the man's hand, I put them down on the counter and let him pick them up himself."

As the impact of her small deed hit her full force, she began to cry. "Look at what those blue scissors did. They cut up the decree against our child."

Rav Elimelech Biderman, the author of the sefer Be'er HaChaim, told the above story, and added a point from Rav Dessler. Sometimes, a miracle needs only a small act or kabbalah (commitment) to allow it to work. It was Mrs. Rothman's small act of tzniyus that opened the door for her son's recovery.

"I wish I could tell you the real name of the child," Rav Biderman concluded. "He is no longer a child, but a chashuve [important] ben Torah [person who is involved in Torah study], who learns in Yeshivas Chevron. Those scissors are prominently displayed in his breakfront."

Hard to imagine anything more valuable.

PREPARED TO FIGHT

The Tzemach Tzedek related the following story, which carries a pertinent message for today's generation.

BORIS WAS BARELY 16 YEARS OLD WHEN HE WAS TAKEN to serve in Czar Nicholas's army. Although keeping the mitzvos while in the company of hundreds of non-Jewish soldiers was a daunting challenge, Boris managed as best as he could. He was careful to eat only kosher food and to avoid desecrating the Shabbos as much as was possible. Each day, he would steal away for a few moments in order to pray: all without the knowledge of his fellow soldiers. If they found out that he was Jewish, they would stop at nothing to make his life miserable.

One day, as was his custom, Czar Nicholas came to Boris's unit to inspect the troops. The soldiers stood at attention, with their guns at their sides, as the czar walked by each one. From time to time, he would stop and ask a soldier a question or two. When he passed Boris, he asked the young man a few questions, including his age and his origin. Upon hearing that Boris was only 16 years old, the czar seemed impressed that such a young boy could hold his own in the army. As he continued to ask him questions, each bright and well-thought answer brought a bigger smile to his face.

The czar felt an attachment to the young man and asked him if he would join him as one of his personal guards, with the appropriate monetary compensation, of course. He would be like his adopted child. Obviously, this would lead the way to a life of power, prestige, and prominence in the political arena. But before Boris even had a chance to respond, Nicholas informed him that if he was not an observant Christian, he would have to convert to Christianity in order to attain the coveted position. Sensing the boy's hesitation, Czar Nicholas asked Boris if he was Jewish. When the boy answered in the affirmative, a wily smile formed on Czar Nicholas's lips as he asked him if he would convert. Although Boris had no intention of converting, he was so intimidated by the czar's presence that he did not know how to respond. When he remained silent, the czar took this as agreement.

The czar immediately ordered his guards to take the boy along with them. Poor Boris did not even have a chance to protest; he joined the czar's caravan and set out for the palace. During the trip to the palace, which took nearly half a day, Boris was silent the entire time. He felt scared and alone, and ashamed that he had not had the courage to protest.

As soon as Boris arrived, exhausted and confused, he was told that he would be undergoing a training course, to learn the rules of his new position. He would learn all about security protocol and the basics of etiquette, as well as how to conduct himself around other heads of state.

Finally, Boris was shown to his room. As soon as the door closed, he began to cry and let the tears flow freely. Although he was a soldier who had already fought in battle, he felt as vulnerable and helpless as a small child. Holed up in his corner, he wished that he were back home. But it was too late for that. He needed to find the strength from within in order to overcome this particular challenge.

He always kept a small copy of the *Tanya* in his backpack. Now, he pulled it out, hoping to find some sort of solace and comfort in the words. As he began to read, his tears still clouded his vision. Nonetheless, he managed to read the words of the Baal HaTanya, Rav Shneur Zalman of Liadi, in which he says (*Likkutei Amarim,* Chapters 14,18) that even people who have sinned so much that they are considered the *kal she'bekalim,* the lowest of the low, can still sacrifice themselves for the sake of Heaven.

As Boris read these words, he was inspired to do what was right. Yes, he knew that his failure to protest and to refuse to convert may have classified him as one of the lowest of the low. But he could still sacrifice himself *al kiddush Hashem,* for the sanctification of G-d. He promised himself that he would not fail twice.

The next day, the czar came to check on him and informed him that a special day was planned. A new contingent of soldiers was going to be inducted into the czar's army, and he had decided that this would be the perfect occasion for Boris to convert, right in front of the young troops. To commemorate the momentous event, the czar had ordered a long procession, much larger than his normal procession. He wanted as much pomp and circumstance as possible.

Indeed it would be a memorable day, but not in the manner Czar Nicholas had planned.

When the guards came to fetch Boris, he was ready to go. They were impressed at his eagerness, as they didn't expect him to be so cooperative. Pleased at his enthusiastic attitude, they put him at the head of the procession, in the same carriage as the czar.

The installation was to take place on a large bridge that crossed into the city; the bridge would provide a fitting platform for the memorable occasion. The czar stepped out of his carriage, and hundreds of his future soldiers stood before him, ready to be inducted into his army. Suddenly, they watched in disbelief as Boris jumped out of the carriage and ran to the edge of the bridge. The czar, in a state of utter panic, screamed for Boris to get down.

He warned him that he was embarrassing the czar and he would pay for his crimes.

But Boris did not care; his mind was set on sanctifying Hashem's Name. He called out to the crowd, "My name is Boris and I am a Jew. A few days ago, the czar promised me riches, fame, and power if I would convert to his religion. I acted like a coward and was unable to refuse. But now, I have built up the courage to say: Never! I will never give up my religion!"

He looked defiantly at the czar one last time and called out, "*Shema Yisrael Hashem Elokeinu Hashem Echad.*"

With that, Boris jumped into the raging river. He was immediately swept away, never to be heard from again.

The Tzemach Tzedek added, "After Boris gave up his life and sanctified the Name of Hashem, there was a big tumult in Heaven. The Heavenly Court convened to decide how Boris should be welcomed to his rightful place. In place of the procession that he had given up, which would have led him to a life of fortune and fame as an adopted child of the czar, a procession would line up at the gates of Heaven to welcome him to a life of honor as a child of the Al-mighty.

"In addition, since Boris was inspired to give up his life through the words of the *Tanya*, the Heavenly Court decreed that the *sefer*'s author, Rav Shnuer Zalman of Liadi, would lead the procession and dance in front of Boris as he was brought into the highest spheres of Heaven."

Rav Schwab often stated that our generation is not faced with the challenge of giving up our lives, as was the case in previous generations. We are fortunate to live in a society in which we are granted freedom of religion and the ability to live peacefully among our neighbors.

However, Rav Schwab would point out, our challenge is no less important. Our test is to sacrifice our minds and our hearts. The influences of secular society are so powerful that they are pulling away our youth by appealing to their hearts and minds. With no less dedication than our ancestors, we must be prepared to sacrifice.

It may mean facing the imposing pressure of peers or the snickering sarcasm of our supposed friends when we try to act more religious. Yet it is all worth it.

One day, there will be a procession — as the leaders of past generations will welcome all those who sacrificed for the sake of Hashem — into the highest spheres of Heaven.

TEFILLAH

WHY DIDN'T I?

Prior to the onset of World War II, a group of Jewish activists arranged for kindertransports, in which 10,000 children from countries such as Germany and Austria were brought to safer locations. Many of these children were taken to London and to villages throughout England, where they were placed in homes or in orphanages, to be cared for and protected.

A few years ago, BBC Radio conducted a live interview with someone who had been on one of those transports, when he was 12 years old. When he was interviewed, the man was well into his 80's. During the course of the interview, as he began to feel more and more comfortable with his interviewers, he told a story with a strong message.

WHEN THE CHILDREN FIRST ARRIVED IN ENGLAND, they felt frightened and alone, as they missed their families terribly, and some of them cried incessantly. But after days and weeks of encouragement, and even bribery, the children became acclimated and tried to make the best of their situation.

There was one boy, however, whom we'll call Daniel, who would not settle down in the orphanage, no matter what his caregivers tried. They gave him candy and toys, but he could not be consoled. Finally, someone asked him what it would take for him to stop crying. He said very clearly that he wanted — no, demanded — a private meeting with the king of England!

Daniel was told that the necessary arrangements would be made, but that if he was going to meet the king, he would have to prepare beforehand. He would have to practice walking, talking, and conducting himself with the etiquette that is proper when meeting royalty. The boy was willing to do whatever was necessary to merit a private meeting with the king. And so, he spent the next three weeks faithfully following all of the instructions, and preparing for this auspicious meeting.

King George VI, a highly unlikely successor to the monarchy, had been crowned in 1937. He had a terrible stutter and other physical ailments, but when his brother abdicated the throne, he became king. Toward the beginning of his reign, he visited many villages, hamlets, and cities so he could get to know the people and see what they needed. He wanted to reassure them, even during those harrowing times, that the country would be safe and secure.

The big day finally arrived. Daniel went to the middle of the town square and stood behind a big barricade. But as the people gathered around and the street filled, he realized that he had been fooled; it would be almost impossible to have a private audience with the king. Instead, he was merely going to wave at the royal carriage when it passed by, just like everyone else. But that was not what he had asked for!

He waited until the royal carriage passed right where he was standing, and before anyone had a chance to stop him, he jumped the barricade and ran with all of his might toward the king's carriage. As soon as the royal guards saw Daniel running toward the carriage, they pounced on him, tackled him to the ground, and then handcuffed him.

Daniel's unsuccessful attempt to reach the king caused quite a commotion — all the way up to the king himself. He looked out of his carriage window and saw the guards on top of the boy, and called out for them to let the boy go. When the guards informed the king of what had happened, he invited Daniel into the carriage. The boy dusted off his clothing, stood up to his full height, and approached the king with admiration.

"Young man," the king addressed Daniel, "why did you run toward the carriage? Is there something you would like to tell me?" At first, the young foreigner was too intimidated to speak. With a bit of coaxing he gained some confidence and began to address the king, his heavily accented speech revealing a little of his background. He told the king that he had been brought to England a few weeks ago, and that he missed his parents so badly that the ache in his heart would not go away.

The king listened with great patience; he knew what it was like to have difficulty expressing oneself, and he sympathized with his new friend. "Now, tell me what you want. I am the king of England and I can do anything for you."

Daniel mustered up the courage to tell the king the purpose of his meeting. "I want you to bring my parents over from Germany."

King George was taken aback. He was prepared for just about anything, but he was not prepared for this. "You do know that we are at war with Germany. It is impossible to bring your parents here."

But the child shot back, "But you're the king of England and you told me you can do anything. Please, please bring my parents to me."

The king looked at the boy's eyes as they filled with tears. "Please don't cry. I promise I will do my utmost to make it happen."

Daniel thanked King George and walked away, somewhat hopeful but unsure about what to expect.

A few days later, there was a knock at the door of the orphanage. Daniel's parents had arrived. Somehow, someway, they were brought out of Germany and reunited with their son.

The BBC reporter watched as the survivor finished his incredible story. Suddenly, the man began to cry. As he wiped the tears from his eyes, he began muttering to himself, "I will never forgive myself. I will never forgive myself."

The reporter did not understand. "What is wrong? That was such a beautiful story. For what won't you forgive yourself?"

The survivor took a deep breath and began to explain. "We all had a chance. Why didn't I, too, jump the barricade? Why didn't I ask the king? Why didn't I save my parents? Why didn't I …?"

Often, the Al-mighty leaves His "palace" and roams throughout the "villages and hamlets" to meet His subjects. But instead of taking advantage of the opportunity and jumping the "barricade," we remain right where we are, and we lose out on the opportunity to ask Him for anything we need.

Let's not lose our chance. Let us not find ourselves crying and wondering, "Why didn't I jump the barricade? Why didn't I ask the King?"

THE COURT CASE

The following awe-inspiring story took place during the time of Rav Aryeh Leib, the Shpolya Zeide. It speaks to our ability to beseech the Al-mighty and voice our frustrations and concerns.

THE SHPOLYA ZEIDE LED HIS CHASSIDIM DURING A DIFficult period. There was a famine in the Ukraine, and the Jews in all the surrounding areas were suffering. The Zeide accepted upon himself to support all the widows and orphans, the poor and impoverished, and any other suffering Jews. He was more than a Rebbe; he was a father. Not a day went by in which people did not come to his home, banging on the door and crying; their children were begging for bread, and they did not have what to feed them. Although he, too, suffered from hunger, he would not put more than a morsel of bread into his mouth when so many others were starving.

As the months passed, the famine spread throughout Russia, and Jews from other villages also found themselves in dire straits. They turned to their leaders, who wrote to the Shpolya Zeide and begged for his help. They asked him to use his power of prayer to plead on behalf of the thousands of starving Jews.

The Zeide, in turn, reached out to many other *gedolim* and asked them to daven. Then he asked for three of them — Rav Zisha of Anipoli, Rav Yaakov of Shapitovka, and Rav Zev Wolf of Zhitomir — to come immediately to Shpolya. When the three of them arrived, the Zeide addressed them with concern. "*Rabbosai*, I asked you to come to the city because I am taking someone to a *din Torah* [judgment in Jewish court], and I want you to be the *dayanim* [judges]."

They asked the name of the defendant and were stunned by the reply. "It is the *Ribbono Shel Olam* Himself. If you are wondering how I could possibly take the Al-mighty to court, the *pasuk* tells us that when it comes to matters of judgment, we should not fear anyone. That includes even the Al-mighty when He is the defendant!

"The law dictates that the claimant must go to the defendant, but there is not one inch of the world that is not filled with His Presence. Therefore, we can have the *din Torah* right here."

The community members gathered in the main *beis midrash,* and the *shamash* announced in a trembling voice, "Rav Aryeh Leib ben Rachel is taking *Hashem Yisbarach* to a *din Torah*. The *din Torah* will begin in this room in three days from now."

For three days, the entire community fasted. They davened, cried, and stormed the Heavens, begging for mercy. Immediately following davening on the fourth day, the four *tzaddikim* entered the room, each wrapped in *tallis* and *tefillin*.

The Zeide began to speak. "In the name of the starving *Yiddishe* women and children of Russia, I am bringing the *Aibeshter* to *din*. Why won't He give them food to eat? Why has He decreed that they must die of hunger?

"It says in His precious Torah [*Vayikra* 25:55], '*Ki li Vnei Yisrael avadim, avadai heim* –For the Children of Israel are servants to Me, they are My servants.' So we see that the Jewish people have at least the status of Jewish servants. The law is that a master must provide food and sustenance for his servant's wife and children. When this Master does not provide for them, He makes a mockery of His Torah, *chas ve'shalom*!

"I know that the Al-mighty may claim that we have not been deserving of His support and sustenance, because we are not proper servants. But there are ways to refute that claim. First of all, just because the servant is not doing his job properly doesn't mean that his wife and his children should starve. Second, it is possible that the servants are not working properly because of the Master Himself. He gives each servant a *yetzer hara,* which can be impossible to deal with, and which prevents us from serving Him properly. He places before us challenges that are seemingly insurmountable. I guarantee that if not for the *yetzer hara,* every Jew would serve his Master perfectly."

The Zeide finished his plea, and the judges huddled together. After a few moments, they proclaimed, "The *din* is with Rav Aryeh Leib ben Rachel, and the Al-mighty is obligated to support and feed the wives and the children of Russian Jewry. Just as we have decided in the courts below, so should it be decided in the Heavenly Court Above."

They made their declaration three times. When they finished, the Zeide took out some small glasses and drank a *le'chaim,* and they sat down and ate a special meal. Toward evening, each of them was on his way.

Five days later, the government announced that the ban restricting wheat and other grains from being transported from Siberia would be lifted. Within days, the streets were full of grains and bread, enough to feed everyone in the country. Because of the overwhelming supply of grain, the price dropped dramatically and everyone was able to feed his family properly.

Some people may question the seeming chutzpah of this story, but great people had a unique relationship with HaKadosh Baruch Hu. In their love for Klal Yisrael, and as they carried the burden of thousands on their shoulders, they would sometimes cry out in pain to their Father in Heaven. At times like these, He would excuse their brashness and grant their requests, for their main desire was to serve Him as perfect servants.

THE SOUND OF SILENCE

The Jewish people have so many tzaros. We cry out in pain and suffering, begging the Al-mighty to have mercy on us. All too often, though, our tefillos don't even have a chance — because of our lack of respect for the holiness of a shul, which causes us to speak during davening and during krias haTorah.

I was recently asked to speak at Agudath Israel Bais Binyomin for an organization that promotes kedushas beis haknesses (the holiness of places of worship). In researching this important subject matter, I came across a terrifying tale from Rav Yeshayah Cheshin, who told this story in front of Rav Yehoshua Leib Diskin and Rav Tzvi Michel Shapiro, both of whom confirmed its authenticity.

A PLAGUE BROKE OUT IN THE TOWN OF OSTRAHA. Though the doctors had tried various treatments, nothing had helped and it seemed as if nothing more could be done. The doctors threw up their hands in desperation, as the plague claimed victim after victim. The rabbanim announced that if anyone knew the reason for this plague, he should come forward and let them know. The city was full of good people. Its inhabitants learned diligently and prayed with great concentration. Countless acts of kindness were performed by young and old alike. No one seemed to have the answer.

Finally, two men decided to follow the activities of one individual who never came to shul. One evening, they stood outside his home and waited for him to emerge, and then they followed him into the forest. It was late at night and the forest was pitch-black. As they began to follow him deeper and deeper into the forest, they became afraid that perhaps he was involved with some sort of a gang, and so they decided to retreat. The next morning, they told their rav about their findings; they were certain that this man was involved in shady dealings. The rav said that the next time the man goes into the forest, they should immediately inform the rav, and he will go with them to discover what this fellow is up to.

Later that night, they waited outside the man's home once again. As soon as he came out of his house and headed toward the forest, they ran to inform the rav. Immediately, the three of them followed him. This time, when they came to the dense part of the forest, they didn't retreat. Instead, they watched with trepidation and awe as he made a fire and began to cry loudly. But his voice was not the only one that was heard. As he cried, another voice joined him and the two of them wept together. Their sobs were bitter and they wailed deep into the night.

The three observers realized that this was no ordinary individual. The next morning, they approached him and asked about the previous night's events. He told them that every night, he mourns the destruction of the *Beis HaMikdash*. The other voice they were hearing was the voice of Yirmiyah HaNavi, who joins him to cry over the *churban* (destruction). They listened with rapt attention to this hidden *tzaddik,* and they asked him if he was aware of the cause of the plague. He assured them that he knew the reason, and that he would share it with everyone. The following morning, the entire community came to shul to hear what the man had to say.

As he stood in the corner of the shul and davened, many people fainted. After davening, he explained to the rav that people had fainted because of his *tefillin,* which are meant to instill fear, as it says, "*Ve'ra'u kol amei ha'aretz ki Sheim Hashem nikra Alecha ve'yaru mimeka* — Then all the peoples of the earth will see that the Name of Hashem is proclaimed over you, and they will revere you" (*Devarim* 28:10). Unfortunately, other people's *tefillin* do not instill fear because people speak while wearing them, and this causes the *tefillin* to lose their extra holiness.

His tone became even more serious as he said to the rav, "This plague has been wreaking havoc because none of your constituents' prayers are answered; and that is happening only because they speak during davening."

Since he did not want to associate with people who speak in shul, he felt that it would be best if he would daven at home. "But if you are willing to take to heart what I have said, and stop speaking in shul, especially with your *tefillin* on, then the plague will stop immediately."

The hidden *tzaddik* finished his speech and the rav wept. He stood up in front of his *kehillah* and shared the *tzaddik's* words with them. The audience cried bitter tears, sensing the severity of their actions. Many had lost loved ones, while others had family members who were on the brink of death. Then they all listened to a fiery *derashah* from the rav, reiterating all that had been said about *kedushas beis haknesses*.

A few days later, the heartrending *tefillos* of the city of Ostroha ascended to Heaven unimpeded by the destructive clouds of spiritual pollution. Their prayers achieved their desired effect; the plague stopped and the community was saved.

We struggle to find solutions to our problems, while there may be a single solution to all of them.
Silence.

ETCHED IN STONE

The Avnei Nezer, Rav Avraham Borenstein, also known as the Sochatchover Rebbe, was a tremendous talmid chacham. His Iglei Tal and other works are classics. His son, Rav Shmuel, who is more widely known as the Shem MiShmuel, was also an outstanding scholar.

Both father and son were very devoted to their Chassidim and to teaching Torah. In addition, their Chassidim turned to them in times of desperation and need. More often than not, when the Rebbe gave his berachah, his words were fulfilled. But one thing was certain: he always gave a berachah.

Except for one case.

MEIR AND HIS WIFE SARAH SUFFERED MANY YEARS without children, and longed to hold a baby in their arms. However, no matter how many times he begged for a blessing from the Avnei Nezer, Meir always came away empty-handed. He and Sarah could not understand it. Why wouldn't the Rebbe give them a *berachah*?

Before every Yom Tov, when he would go to spend time with the Rebbe, as he bid his wife farewell she would remind him not to leave without receiving his blessing. The Rebbe would give him *berachos* for riches and health, but never for a child. One time, he built up the chutzpah to ask the Rebbe why he never gave him a blessing for a child.

The Rebbe sat quietly for a long while. Then he looked at his devoted Chassid, and it was obvious that he felt his pain. Nevertheless, he had a reason for refusing, and it was legitimate. Finally, he decided to reveal his reason, so he turned back to Meir and asked his dispirited Chassid pointedly, "Do you want to have a child who is going to be a priest?"

Meir was shaken to the core. With complete faith in his Rebbe's sharp and ominous words, he never asked again. He accepted his lonely and bitter fate; he and his wife were meant to be without children. They would rather have no children than a child who would become a priest!

Many years passed and the Avnei Nezer passed away. His son, the Shem MiShmuel, became his successor and Meir's new Rebbe. Meir continued the custom of spending Yom Tov with his mentor, but kept to his commitment not to ask for a blessing for a child. One Yom Tov, as he was about to bid farewell to his new Rebbe, he was surprised when the Shem MiShmuel asked, "Why don't you ask me for a blessing for a son? You have languished in loneliness for so many years."

Meir did not know how to respond. His insides screamed silently, Yes, Rebbe, please bless us with the child for whom we yearn. But he knew better than to test fate. The Avnei Nezer had seemed to intuit that a child of his would bring about a *chillul Hashem* (desecration of Hashem's Name). If that was the case, he didn't want a child! But the Shem MiShmuel saw his tears, blessed him and told him, that he would daven for him to have a child.

Meir wanted to beg the Rebbe to take back his words, but it was too late. Despite their concern, when Meir and his wife were miraculously blessed with a child after nearly 20 years of marriage, they allowed themselves to rejoice. Amazingly, over the next five years, they had four more children. Still, Meir had his reservations; the Avnei Nezer's warnings echoed in his mind. His child was destined to become a priest. How could he be completely happy?

Their eldest, Avraham, named after the Avnei Nezer, was a delightful child. Though he grew up with the other children in the village, his parents and rebbeim recognized that he was unique. Gifted and talented, he soared to the top of his classes. Yet, as he grew older, ominous clouds appeared in the sky. Europe was engulfed in war and it wasn't long before their village was targeted for destruction. Avraham's parents sensed the imminent danger and tried their best to escape, but it was too late.

The Nazis advanced upon the town, killing Meir and Sarah, along with all of the inhabitants of the village. Only one person, Avraham, miraculously survived. He managed to find shelter in a monastery, and through the kindness of one of the men in charge was able to pose as a priest!

It was not easy. The Nazis made their way into the monastery searching for Jews. They were not easily persuaded that Avraham was a priest. However, as a gifted linguist, he was able to converse in many languages and put on a good show. Eventually, the Nazis were convinced and left him alone.

When the war was over, he made his way out of Europe and moved to Israel, where he picked up the pieces of his destroyed life and established a family.

The blessing of the Shem MiShmuel had come true. And the words of his father, the Avnei Nezer, had also come true. Meir's son had become a priest, but it was only as a disguise. Indeed, it may have been decreed that Avraham was going to be a priest, but nothing is etched in stone. And the power of prayer is immense.

Our challenges may be different and may sound somewhat less dramatic. Yet the power of prayer remains the same.

Nothing is certain in life. No one is doomed to a life of failure and misery.

Not when the power of tefillah — and the tears that accompany it — exist.

A Glowing Report

Even when we feel content with our current state of affairs, we should never take the situation for granted, nor should we stop pouring out our hearts in prayer. Sometimes, all HaKadosh Baruch Hu wants is our sincere and heartfelt tefillos.

The following story illustrates this point in a striking manner.

MOISHELE, A CHASSIDISHE AMERICAN *BACHUR*, WAS learning in the Gerrer Yeshivah, Sfas Emes, in Yerushalayim. Although it was not easy for him to be away from home, Moishele learned diligently and put a tremendous amount of effort into his *avodas Hashem* and into his learning. He got along very well with his peers, and they held him in high esteem. His perseverance, diligence, and *middos* did not go unnoticed. The Pnei Menachem, the rosh yeshivah at the time, took a liking to him and enjoyed speaking with him in learning.

One day, the young man's father, Reb Yeshaya, came from America to visit. He received outstanding reports from his son's rebbeim. He met a number of Moishele's friends and was able to sense the admiration they had for his son. He went to the Pnei Menachem and asked how his son was doing, eager to elicit another "*nachas* report." Surprisingly, when he introduced himself, the Pnei Menachem gave a very lukewarm response.

Reb Yeshaya was disappointed and was prepared to walk away, dejected. Then he realized that he had not said that he was the father of Moishele; perhaps the Pnei Menachem had not realized he was the boy's father, and that was why Reb Yeshaya had not been acknowledged and had not received a glowing report. He went back to the rosh yeshivah and made sure to mention that he was the father of Moishele. Once again, the Pnei Menachem acted indifferently. This time, the silence was deafening. Reb Yeshaya was bewildered.

Doubts began creeping in. Was there something that he did not know about his child? Did the Pnei Menachem have some sort of knowledge that prevented him from thinking positively about Moishele? No longer able to hold in his concerns, Reb Yeshaya came straight to the point. "I know my son is a good boy. I asked everyone in the yeshivah about him, and they were all very impressed. The rosh yeshivah seems to be deliberately avoiding any praise. Is there a reason the rosh yeshivah does not want to give me a favorable report about my son? Is there something I should know about my child?"

The Pnei Menachem understood Reb Yeshaya's disappointment. Which father doesn't want to hear praise about his child? In order to explain why he was silent, he told the following story.

Before World War II, there was a decree drafting yeshivah boys into the Polish army. When the time came for my brother, who grew up under the tutelage of the Imrei Emes, to be drafted into the army, my mother went to the Imrei Emes and asked if he could promise that her son would not be drafted.

To her shock, the Imrei Emes was silent. He did not promise anything. She took this as a sign that her son was going to serve in the army, and she began to cry bitterly about her child's future.

When her mother saw her crying, she went over to her son-in-law, the Imrei Emes, and told him how distraught her daughter was and how much she was crying. At that moment, the Rebbe assured his mother-in-law that there was nothing to worry about because the young man was not going to be drafted. His mother-in-law immediately gave her daughter the wonderful news.

But one thing bothered her: Why had the Imrei Emes waited to share the important news? When she posed the question to the Rebbe, his response spoke volumes. "Ah mamma darf veinen — A mother needs to cry. Had I told her immediately that he was going to be exempt, she would not have cried for his overall well-being and safety.

"The tears shed by a Yiddishe mamma are precious and valuable. Her son may not have needed those tears right now, but he will certainly need them in the future. It is for this reason that I delayed in reassuring her that he would not have to serve in the army."

The Pnei Menachem explained, "When you asked me how your son was doing, I could have told you immediately how outstanding he is. However, you would have felt content and comfortable. When one does not feel a need to daven for his child, he will not be shedding a parent's precious tears.

"As wonderful as your child is, don't ever stop crying on his behalf."

FOUND AND LOST – AND FOUND AGAIN

TZVIKA ENJOYED PURCHASING A NEW *SIDDUR* EVERY once in a while. One day, as he left shul, he saw a man selling *siddurim*, and the man encouraged him to buy a *Siddur HaRashash*, a *siddur* with the commentary of Rav Shalom Sharabi. Although Tzvika was not into Kabbalah, the *siddur* he had purchased is one of the main *siddurim* used by Kabbalists.

Tzvika made it a point to visit the holy places in Eretz Yisrael. He enjoyed going to the Kosel, Kever Rachel, Me'aras HaMachpeilah, and to the many *kevarim* (graves) scattered across Eretz Yisrael. During these visits, he davened from the *Siddur HaRashash*. He didn't understand any of its deeper *kavannos* (intentions). Yet he hoped that since he was using such a holy *siddur,* his simple recitation of the words carried with it some extra meaning.

One time, he traveled up north to visit the *kever* of Rabbi Shimon bar Yochai, the Rashbi. He had a lot on his mind and wanted to pour out his heart in prayer. Only a few months before, his sister had lost her husband, and she was left alone with three small orphans. He spent the day up north and headed home, hopeful that his *tefillos* had been accepted.

Two weeks later, Tzvika received a phone call from a fellow named Chaggai Ben Shimon. Tzvika racked his brain, trying to remember how he may have known him, but the man assured him that he didn't. He was calling to inform Tzvika that he had his *siddur*.

Tzvika was surprised. Now that he thought about it, though, he remembered that he had not seen his *siddur* lately. When he tried to think of the last time he had used it, he realized that it must have been when he had davened at the *kever* of Rabbi Shimon bar Yochai. He was grateful that Chaggai had taken the time and made the effort to track him down. "I will tell you the truth," he said to Chaggai. "I am very appreciative that you called me, but I would like you to keep my *siddur*. Without you, I would never have found it anyway. I sense that you are the type of person who is probably more worthy of using it than I am."

Chaggai thanked his newfound friend for his gesture and told him that regardless, he would be happy to meet Tzvika the next time that he went up north. Two weeks later, Tzvika went back to the *kever* of the Rashbi — his sister asked him to, as she needed some *chizuk* — and he met Chaggai. They struck up a nice conversation and committed to be in touch with each other.

Two years passed; neither heard from the other.

One day, Tzvika's phone rang. "Is this Tzvika?" When Tzvika answered in the affirmative, the caller said, "I just want you to know that we have your *tefillin*."

Tzvika informed the man that he had not lost his *tefillin,* but the caller insisted that he was holding a set of *tefillin* that was found along with a *Siddur HaRashash,* which contained his name and number. The man identified himself as Armand from the Akko police station. Until recently, he explained, an Arab had been running the lost-and-found office, but now, he had taken over and was going through some of the old items. Tzvika realized what had happened, and he also knew who owned the set of *tefillin.*

He tried to call Chaggai, but there was no answer. He made some inquiries, but no one seemed to know Chaggai's whereabouts; he seemed to have vanished into thin air. Armand had said that the *tefillin* had been in their possession for the last two years. This really concerned Tzvika. What in the world had happened to Chaggai?

Eventually, Tzvika decided to pick up the *tefillin* himself. He traveled to Akko, thanked Armand for his efforts, took the *tefillin* and the *siddur,* and headed out toward a hotel for the night. Since he was not so far from Tzfas, he decided to use the opportunity to daven at the Arizal's shul in the morning.

He woke up early the next morning and davened at the *neitz* (sunrise) *minyan*. When he saw the *chazzan* turn around, Tzvika was utterly shocked. There he was, in the flesh: Chaggai Ben Shimon!

"You are not going to believe this," he said to Chaggai after davening. "I have something that I want to give to you." And he handed him the bag with the *tefillin* and the *siddur*. Chaggai held them close to his heart; tears sprang to his eyes.

Tzvika told him how he had tried to contact him over the past few weeks, but was unsuccessful. What had happened? Where had he gone?

"Thank you so much for looking out for me," said Chaggai. "The past two years have been extremely difficult. First, my car was stolen. Then, I came down with a serious heart ailment. During this time, I lost my *tallis* and *tefillin* as well. In fact, I have not yet purchased a new set, as I was always hopeful I would find my old ones.

"I was wondering what else could possibly go wrong. At the end of the two years, my wife was killed in a car accident. My life fell apart completely. I was broken and shattered beyond measure, unable to care for my two sons. My brother-in-law and his family, and my brother and his family, helped me care for my children and stabilize my life. They are such caring people."

Chaggai took out the *siddur* and held it in his hands. "But I have no questions on the Al-mighty. I only have questions about myself."

After hugging Chaggai goodbye, Tzvika was shaken up. How sad it was that his friend's life had fallen apart over the last two years.

That night, Tzvika could not fall sleep. Suddenly, he jumped out of bed. *That's it,* he thought to himself. *Chaggai is such a wonderful person. And my sister is a wonderful young woman. They both need a shidduch.*

He didn't even wait until morning. He called both parties right then. Within a short amount of time, the two met. They both agreed with Tzvika that the match was perfect, and before long they were married.

At the wedding, Tzvika spoke about the *Hashgachah* involved in the *shidduch*. How Chaggai had called to return his *Siddur HaRashash,* and how that had set everything in motion. Above all, Tzvika felt it was important to share a penetrating thought, one that carries with it a timely message.

The Siddur HaRashash contains many deep and mystical kavannos, which are beyond the comprehension of most individuals. Nevertheless, we use the siddur and recite the words with their simplest meaning, hoping that we may catch a glimpse of the intended kavannos.

In a similar vein, HaKadosh Baruch Hu orchestrates this world with a "seder," the word "seder" having the same root as the word "siddur." Though we may not comprehend the infinite wisdom of the Al-mighty — as we are mere mortals whose lives are directed from above — every once in a while we catch a glimpse of His "intentions."

DON'T JUDGE A JEW BY HIS (HEAD) COVER

As the waves of assimilation washed over German Jewry in the early part of the 20th century, many Jews intermarried and were lost to the Jewish people forever. As such, German Jews were very sensitive about tampering with their traditions.

R AV YECHIEL YAAKOV WEINBERG HEADED THE Hildesheimer Rabbinical Seminary in Berlin. He authored a *sefer* of halachic responsa, *Seridei Eish*, and was revered worldwide for his brilliance and erudition. He educated hundreds of students and left an indelible impression on them. He was fluent in a number of languages and knowledgeable in worldly matters, as well. With his impeccable German, Rav Weinberg was a very sought-after speaker.

When World War II broke out, Rav Weinberg was imprisoned along with Russian prisoners of war. After the war, he joined one of his closest *talmidim*, Rav Shaul Weingort, in the city of Montreux, Switzerland. He was offered positions around the globe, but he chose to remain there until he died.

Rav Weingort once gave a *shiur* in the city of Modi'in, Israel, on the topic of honoring one's parents. It was attended by a large crowd, all of whom enjoyed the lecture immensely. He punctuated his points with a memorable story about his rebbi.

> *Many Jews davened each week in the central synagogue in Berlin. On the Yamim Noraim [High Holidays], there was an especially large crowd. Although it was a long walk for Rav Weinberg, he made sure to daven in the main synagogue on Rosh Hashanah and Yom Kippur. The worshipers were honored by his presence, and they gave him a prominent seat along the eastern wall.*
>
> *Every year on Yom Kippur, after the morning services and the reading of the Torah, the gabbai announced in a loud and clear voice, "Yizkor!" With this announcement, many of the younger members of the synagogue, whose parents were still alive, went outside into the hallway and spilled out onto the steps in front of the synagogue. When the room was free of all non-orphans, the doors were closed and the orphans began reciting the emotional prayer of Yizkor.*
>
> *One Yom Kippur in the early 1920's, just as the crowd*

gathered in front of the synagogue, a black limousine pulled up in front of the building, with one police car in front and one bringing up the rear.

The door of the limousine swung open and out stepped the distinguished-looking, bareheaded politician, industrial magnate, and author named Walther Rathenau. At the time, he also served as the foreign minister of the Weimar Republic. Rathenau was a controversial figure. The non-Jews didn't like him because he was Jewish, and the Jews were wary of him because he was assimilated.

He walked right past the crowd and made his way toward the main sanctuary. When Rathenau entered, he was gratified to discover that he had come in time for Yizkor. As he stepped into the sanctuary, however, a commotion ensued outside. Why was Walther Rathenau coming to shul on Yom Kippur, and how dare he walk in without a head covering? Many of the congregants were furious. Did he really think that just show-ing up in shul would absolve him of all the sins he had com-mitted? Some people defended him and told the rabble-rousers to mind their own business.

When Yizkor was over, Rathenau walked out of the build-ing, stepped back into his car, and was chauffeured away. Even so, the commotion continued. The chazzan was ready to begin Mussaf, but the crowd was still deliberating whether Rathenau had a right to be there or not.

Finally, Rav Weinberg stood up in front of the crowd and asked for permission to speak. For once, silence filled the room; everyone wanted to hear what he had to say. He stood there for a minute surveying the crowd, and then he spoke in a passionate tone.

"Rabbosai, how can Jews not be afraid to embarrass a Jew who comes to the synagogue with the pure and well-meaning intention of honoring his parents? Somebody who honors the memory of his parents is guaranteed that he and his children *will not be lost to the Jewish people forever."*

When he finished speaking, no one moved and no one stirred. The two-minute speech had made its mark on the congregants.

When Rav Weingort told the story in Modi'in, it made a tremendous impact on his audience, as well. After everyone left, someone came over to speak to the rav. "My father's grandfather was Walther Rathenau. About 20 years ago, my father became a *baal teshuvah*, and I was privileged to grow up as a true Torah Jew."

Rav Weingort listened in amazement. He had witnessed firsthand the fulfillment of his rebbi's guarantee.

THE PURPOSE OF IT ALL

It is really not necessary to tell miraculous tales about Rav Yosef Shalom Elyashiv. The greatest miracle of all was his diligence, his hasmadah, how he learned uninterrupted his entire life. Anyone who ever came in contact with him was awed by his insatiable desire to learn.

Nevertheless, the following story tells of the power of tefillah, and is an apt example of Rav Elyashiv's understanding of the power of all mitzvos, and what obeying them can accomplish.

FOR A LONG TIME, BARUCH, A YOUNG MARRIED FELLOW from the city of Elad, looked forward to a vacation with his family. The children had asked to go to a waterpark, and he was more than happy to take them. At long last, *bein hazmanim* (intersession) arrived, and they were ready to go. After everyone and everything were packed into the van, Baruch started down the road. Suddenly, upon rounding a bend, he noticed that a truck was heading in his direction. He managed to turn the wheel and avoid a head-on collision. Unfortunately, though, the van spun out of control and careened wildly. Then it fell off a cliff and tumbled over numerous times until it finally came to a stop.

Baruch, his wife, Chani, and all their children were shaken up. Nevertheless, though each family member had suffered some sort of injury — there were broken arms, broken legs, fractured ribs, as well as cuts and bruises — no one was critically injured. No one other than 9-year-old Yossi, that is; his injuries were too numerous to count.

From seemingly out of nowhere, ambulances arrived and took all the family members to the hospital. Though they were uncomfortable from their minor injuries, Baruch and Chani could think of nothing but their children. Then, once the rest of their children's injuries had been tended to, they were able to focus all their attention on their beloved Yossi, whose life was hanging in the balance.

He had been taken into surgery immediately, where he underwent a long operation, in which the doctors tried to stabilize him and stop the swelling and bleeding in his brain. While everyone who knew the family prayed on Yossi's behalf, Baruch and Chani waited for word from the surgeon. Would their son make it? Would he be able to live a normal life? The alternatives were too frightening to even contemplate.

After eight interminable hours, the doctors emerged from the operating room and met with the family. They informed Baruch and Chani that Yossi had suffered severe head trauma, and they were very pessimistic. The chance of him pulling through with all his cognitive abilities was slim indeed. The doctors told the shocked parents that the next few days would be crucial. If Yossi woke up within those days, then there would be room for hope. If not —

With a *Tehillim* in their hands at all times, Baruch and Chani kept a vigil next to Yossi's bed in the intensive care unit, never leaving their child for a moment. They spoke to him and sang to him, hoping that what they were saying would make an impression. Family and friends came to visit and brought food and toys. In truth, there was no use for any of the gifts. Baruch and Chani weren't eating — they couldn't think of food at a time like this — and Yossi was in no condition to play with any of the toys. However, their visitors' thoughtfulness and caring were very much appreciated by Yossi's parents.

A few days passed. Once again, Baruch and Chani met with the doctors, who repeated their gloomy prognosis. Since by this time Yossi had not shown any sign of brain activity, the medical team was fairly certain that even if he were to emerge from his comatose state, he would be severely crippled and brain damaged. It was highly doubtful that he would ever function as a normal person again.

Baruch and Chani looked at their son; his head was bandaged and he was almost unrecognizable from all the swelling. There were a myriad of machines attached to him monitoring his every move; his parents never felt more helpless in their lives.

Yossi, with messy black hair and gorgeous blue eyes, was bright, cute, and charming. Everyone who knew him loved him. His rebbeim spoke glowingly about his abilities, and his friends enjoyed playing with him. But now, none of that mattered. His parents could not help but wonder if he would ever go to school again.

Baruch felt guilty that he had been driving the car, and, of everybody, he had suffered the mildest injuries. He would even pray that the Al-mighty should put him in his son's place. He wished that he was the one who was suffering, and that his son was the healthy one. But that is not the way Providence had dictated.

Baruch decided to go with his wife to *gedolim* (sages) to seek *berachos* for Yossi.

He begged each of the *gedolim* to beseech Heaven on his son's behalf. Since it was difficult to get an appointment with some of the *gedolim*, one of Baruch's close friends, an expert *tefillin-macher*, used some of his connections to obtain an audience with Rav Elyashiv. He went himself to speak to the rav, acting as Baruch's representative.

He expected to give Yossi's name to Rav Elyashiv, that Rav Elyashiv would then wish the boy a *refuah sheleimah*, and that he would pray on his behalf. Instead, Rav Elyashiv instructed the *tefillin-macher* to prepare a beautiful pair of *tefillin* for Yossi for his bar mitzvah. The fellow listened carefully to the suggestion, but reminded Rav Elyashiv that the boy was only 9 years old.

Rav Elyashiv just nodded his head; he was aware of the boy's age. He told the man that after he completes the *tefillin*, he should put them in a bag, and he should put that bag next to the child's head.

Without hesitation, the man ran to his home to prepare a pair of *tefillin* for Yossi. When he had completed the *tefillin*, he took them to the hospital. He handed the bag to his friend Baruch and told him the entire story. On top of the bag, he placed a piece of paper, upon which he wrote Yossi's name and the name of his mother, and prayed that this action should bring about Yossi's speedy and complete recovery.

Baruch became very emotional. He could not help but wonder if his child would have the privilege of wearing these *tefillin* at the time of his bar mitzvah. With tears streaming down his face, he took the bag of *tefillin* and placed it gently next to Yossi's head. What a sight to see! Even the nonreligious nurses in the hospital were overcome with emotion, as Yossi's father and mother cried and prayed that their child should one day merit to wear these *tefillin*.

At that very moment, the doctor walked into Yossi's room to tell Baruch and Chani that there was no more hope for Yossi's recovery. Yet Baruch insisted that Hashem runs the world, and He alone would determine whether the child would live or not.

Baruch and Chani sat there and continued to wait. And then, the day after the *tefillin* had been placed at the head of his bed, Yossi opened his eyes. It was an open miracle! The next day, there was further progress. Two weeks later, after continued improvement every day, Yossi was wheeled out of the hospital. Within six months, he was back in yeshivah, functioning like a regular boy.

Baruch and Chani went back to Rav Elyashiv, this time with Yossi, to thank him for his efforts and to show him the fruits of his advice. He was extremely pleased and gave the young man a *berachah* for a long life, filled with good health. He blessed him further that he should bring much *nachas* to his parents and to the *Ribbono Shel Olam*.

Rav Elyashiv also asked that they not publicize the story in his lifetime. And so, the story was known only by those who were intimately involved in the details.

After Rav Elyashiv passed away, Baruch went to the Elyashiv home and related the miraculous story. Rav Elyashiv's family members told Baruch that there were three other instances in which Rav Elyashiv had recommended this segulah for someone with a brain injury. Yossi's case was the fourth and final one.

When Baruch traveled to Bnei Brak to retell the story to Rav Chaim Kanievsky, Rav Elyashiv's son-in-law, Rav Chaim wasn't surprised at all. In fact, he added that the Midrash says that the Al-mighty created a man's head only so that it can wear tefillin. Rav Chaim remarked, "If there are tefillin, then there is a reason for there to be a 'rosh — a head.'"

In a few months from now, Yossi will be celebrating his bar mitzvah. Who can begin to imagine the joy he and his family will experience when he puts on those tefillin for the first time?

As an eighth-grade rebbi, every year I have the privilege of witnessing 75 boys putting on tefillin for the first time. The excitement is palpable. Fathers, uncles, and brothers all come to celebrate the occasion. Occasionally, mothers and sisters will stand in the hallway and try to catch a glimpse of their son or their brother as he dons his tefillin. Proud family members make sure to take pictures and record the occasion for posterity.

My wish to the boys is always the same. I bless each one that when he is his father's age, he should feel the same excitement when donning his tefillin as he feels today.

How special that would be.

HOW MUCH IS IT WORTH?

The following stories connect with the previous one. Even if we have davened many tefillos during the course of our lives, and put on tefillin or have been counted as part of a minyan (quorum) innumerable times, we must always appreciate the value of tefillah, and the value of the mitzvos connected to tefillah.

Indeed, how much is a prayer worth to you? How much is davening with a minyan worth to you? And how much is the mitzvah of tefillin worth to you?

These are questions we must ask ourselves.

In the following two stories, we see how far people will go to daven with a minyan.

KALMAN, A YOUNG AMERICAN, WAS VERY CAREFUL TO daven with a *minyan* three times a day. He once traveled to Eretz Yisrael, and by the time the plane landed and his taxi pulled into Yerushalayim, it was way past midnight. There were no more *minyanim* to be found, even at the famous "*minyan* factory" in Zichron Moshe. Kalman, who was so committed to davening with a *minyan,* was now left without one. What a shame that his first opportunity to daven in Eretz Yisrael would be without a *minyan.*

The taxi driver sensed Kalman's frustration and asked what was bothering him. When Kalman explained his predicament, the driver came up with a radical suggestion; he would gather a *minyan* from among his fellow taxi drivers. Putting action to word, he got onto his walkie-talkie and began summoning his buddies to come together. Within a few moments, 10 cabbies answered the call and met in one central location. Indeed, Kalman had his *minyan*: the most unusual *minyan* he had ever joined!

After *Maariv,* Kalman thanked the drivers profusely and offered to pay their tab, but they refused to take money; they smiled and thanked him for the opportunity to participate in this mitzvah.

The following story was told by Rav Gamliel Rabinovich.

Yanky was driving home from work one evening. While stopped at a red light, his car was struck by a drunken driver. The car was demolished; shattered glass and twisted metal were scattered in the street. Miraculously, Yanky sustained only minor injuries. However, the car's safety bags had deployed, trapping him inside the car. Somehow, he managed to crawl past the airbags and broken windshield, and exit the wrecked vehicle. And not a moment too soon. For just after he emerged, the car went up in flames. As he surveyed the damage, it was obvious to Yanky that he could have been killed.

By then, sirens were screaming their way through the streets, as fire engines, police cars, rescue units, and ambulances rushed to the scene of the accident. Overcome with emotion, Yanky spent a few moments trying to calm down. Then he called his wife and told her what had happened and reassured her that he was all right.

The police investigators asked Yanky to give them all of the details of the accident. He told them that he had been waiting at a red light when another driver came crashing into him. As Yanky interacted with the other driver, it was obvious that the man was drunk. It seemed like a clear, open-and-shut case.

As the investigators continued to methodically record the information, though, Yanky realized that the sun was setting and he would have to rush to make a *minyan* for *Minchah*.

He had always been careful to daven with a *minyan,* and he was not prepared to make an exception today, especially after his miraculous salvation. He asked the policemen if they would wait while Yanky went to a synagogue to pray. The police officers looked at each other, and then they looked back at him; they had never heard such a strange request. They told him that their questions would take another 15-20 minutes, even if they hurried.

Yanky didn't know what to do. He knew that if the police report was not filed properly, he could lose out on the insurance money due him. He could not afford to lose the money for the entire car, but priorities were priorities. He pushed the investigators a bit harder, and they said they would go to their commanding officer and ask him what the protocol should be. Yanky watched as they presented the question to their commanding officer. From his reaction, it was obvious to Yanky that he had no intention of allowing him to leave the scene of the accident.

The commanding officer then approached Yanky and commended him for his commitment to his religion. "Even so," he said, "you first have to finish with the investigators, and then do yourself a favor and go home and rest. You've been through a lot today and no doubt, you are traumatized by the experience. As you know, if you do leave, then you are risking losing all of your insurance money, because without a proper police report you will not be able to file an insurance claim. Are you ready to forfeit all the money you are entitled to?"

Yanky decided to try a different tack. "Let me ask you a question. If you had a meeting right now with a prime minister, head of state, or the president of the United States, what would you do? Would you be able to simply walk away from your meeting? Of course not!"

The officer continued to impress upon him the importance of completing the police report, but Yanky was adamant. He told him that he could not wait anymore. "I know this may sound crazy to you, but if I have to lose out on the insurance claim, then so be it. But I am not willing to miss my *minyan* for *Minchah*. No matter what!"

The officer shook his head and then smiled. "You know, I don't think I would do this for anyone else. We certainly have never done it before. But you seem like a very sincere fellow. Why don't you go pray while we wait here, and we'll complete the rest of the report when you get back."

And that's exactly what happened. The police officers waited for Yanky to catch his *minyan*. They knew how much it meant to him.

Finally, this story drives home the idea of appreciating the mitzvah of tefillin.

Rav Eliyahu Roth, a pious Yerushalmi Yid from the past generation, once approached a *yungerman* (young married fellow), who stood in the corner of the shul with his *tallis* draped over his shoulder as he prepared to don his *tefillin*. Rav Eliyahu said, "*Yungerman*, I have a proposition for you. I can make you some instant money. Leave your *tallis* and *tefillin* here right now and go home, and I will pay you $50."

The man looked at Rav Eliyahu in astonishment. "Do you think that I would ever *not* put on my *tefillin*?"

Rav Eliyahu refused to give up. "O.K. How about if I give you $100? $500? How about $1,000?"

With each question, his persistence increased.

The young fellow became very agitated; he raised his voice and cried out, "I don't know what you want from me. Even if you would leave $1 million on the table, I would still not entertain the thought. I would never even think about it. I put on my *tefillin* every single day since my bar mitzvah, and no money in the world will get me not to."

When Rav Eliyahu heard his response, he smiled. "I will tell you what my intention was, and what I wanted from you. Here you are telling me in no uncertain terms that no matter how much money I give you, even $1 million, you will not give up the privilege of wearing *tefillin* for even one day of your life. So then tell me, please. Why, when I see you putting them on, do I not sense the unimaginable joy that you would have if someone gave you $1 million? If it is worth that much to you, shouldn't you react in the same manner?"

Now that's a great question.

THE REBBE'S AVEIRAH

Rav Yaakov Yitzchak Horowitz was known as the Chozeh of Lublin; he earned this title because of his remarkable intuition. Thousands flocked to him from all over: from the most righteous and most brilliant to the boors and simpletons. When Yidden came to him with their problems, he listened to their

worries and commiserated with them. Through his tefillos and
supplications, he helped bring about their salvation, often in
wondrous ways.

*   The following story is not about a miraculous deliverance.*
Rather, it is about a sin that the Chozeh committed. In fact, we
can learn as much about a tzaddik's greatness from the sins
he claims he has committed as we can from the mitzvos he
performs.

THE CHASSIDIM OF THE CHOZEH WERE CONCERNED about their Rebbe's unusual behavior. He was spending all his time crying in his chamber. No one seemed to know why, and they were all too afraid to go in and ask. Finally, one brave individual stepped forward. He knocked lightly on the door and let himself in.

"Rebbe," he began, "we are worried about you. Why have you been crying? Did we do something wrong? Is there anything we can do stop your tears? Please tell us."

The Rebbe looked at his Chassid, and his eyes were red as he said, "No. It is not because of anything that anyone else has done. I am crying for something that I have done, something dreadful."

The Chassid was even more confused. "Rebbe, what could you have done wrong? You spend your entire day immersed in holiness. You are always learning or praying. The only time you stop is when you are helping others. What makes you say that you sinned?"

The Rebbe would not be put off. "*Oy,* but I have. I talked in the middle of davening. Is that not awful? Is that not a reason to cry?"

Then he proceeded to tell the Chassid about the circumstances behind his sin:

A few days ago, I was already in the middle of my prayers
when a woman suddenly walked into the beis midrash, cry-
ing hysterically. She came running over to me and begged

me, "Rebbe, please help my daughter. She was married for
many years and was never blessed with a child. Then finally,
she became pregnant earlier this year. Now she is in labor, and
the doctors just informed us that neither she nor her baby is
going to live.

"Please, you must do something. I beg of you; don't let a
mother lose her daughter and her grandchild."

The woman couldn't stop crying. I asked her for her name
and her daughter's name, and I promised that I would daven
on their behalf.

"Do you understand?" concluded the Chozeh. "I was *mafsik* [stopped] in the middle of davening!"

The Chozeh was completely distraught, and his Chassid tried to make him feel better. "Yes, but Rebbe, you were doing a mitzvah; you saved her life! That's not an *aveirah*."

The Chozeh appreciated the sentiment but responded, "Just because I was doing a mitzvah doesn't mean that I didn't sin. A *nazir*, who is considered a very holy person, must bring a sacrifice after he completes his *nezirus*, because he sinned when he abstained from wine. Also, if someone is obligated to fast on Shabbos for a specific reason, he must compensate for that by fasting once more in the middle of the week. It is true that he performed a mitzvah, but that does not absolve him from the sin he has committed. So you see, I sinned and that is why I am crying."

The Chassid was humbled by the Chozeh's sincerity and humility, but he still had one more question: "At which point in davening did the woman enter the room?"

The Chozeh responded that she came in while he was in middle of reciting *Hodu*.

The Chassid was even more confused. "But Rebbe, isn't one permitted to speak when he is saying *Hodu*, which is recited before one begins *Baruch She'amar* [for those who daven *Nusach Sefard*]?"

The Chozeh was still not comforted. "Yes, that is true. But for those who daven *Nusach Ashkenaz,* it is forbidden to speak. And that is why I must do *teshuvah.*"

I feel a special attachment to the above story, as the following story and accompanying postscript indicate:

Ten years ago, a video was shown to a group of Israelis who lived in Baltimore and were not yet fully committed to Torah.

On the video, a very sick child appeared on stage, along with Rav Amnon Yitzchak, who challenged the thousands of non-religious Israelis in the audience to accept upon themselves the yoke of Heaven and to repent. The people in the audience were very inspired and moved by the plight of the sick child who stood at the podium. One by one, they stepped forward to make commitments. The men accepted yarmulkes or tzitzis, while the women took scarves with which to cover their hair, or shawls to cover their arms or necks in shows of modesty.

The video showed that a few months later, the sickly boy, who had been dying of cancer, was miraculously cured.

The video was turned off, and a woman named Mrs. Seleh stood in front of the room in the shul in Baltimore. Odeliah, her daughter, was also very sick, and she asked this group to make commitments for her sake.

Then, Odeliah, who was 4 years old at the time, walked into the room. She was bald from her treatments and could walk only with a walker. Yet she had a radiant and brilliant smile, along with a sparkle in her eyes, which spoke to her inner strength and beauty. One by one, the people in the room, too, stepped forward, to take upon themselves mitzvos in Odeliah's merit.

I was very moved by the story and discussed it with Rabbi Zvi Teichman and Rabbi Shragi Herskowitz, two *chashuveh* men with whom I have a close relationship. After I finished the story, they pulled no punches. They said, "Okay, Spero, what are you going to do? What are you going to accept upon yourself in her honor and merit?"

At the time, I was lax about not speaking during davening. Right there and then, I accepted upon myself to refrain from speaking during davening in our *beis midrash*.

Sadly, Odeliah Seleh passed away a year later. Nevertheless, I was not prepared to stop. And now, 10 years later, I still have not spoken in our *beis midrash*. Not one word.

Every year on Shemini Atzeres, Reb Shragi and I share a very special *Kiddush,* in which I reaccept my commitment for another year.

I debated whether to include this addendum or not. I am not writing this to toot my own horn; I certainly have many, many shortcomings, especially regarding my approach to prayer. However, I am hopeful that others will say: "If he can do it, so can I."

And it will serve as a zechus for the neshamah of Odeliah.

If even one person is inspired to act upon these stories or their addendum, it will all be worth it.

EMUNAH

THE HEAD
OF THE PROGRAM

Of the many crises that face the Jewish people today, the shidduchim crisis is one of the most painful, as thousands of young ladies of marriageable age cannot seem to find their proper match. Much has been written about the subject. Many people have suggested solutions. Although all of the suggestions have some validity, there is really only one way to solve this crisis: Emunah. If we believe in Hashem, then there may be frustration and challenge, but whatever happens is really for the best. The following story conveys this message in a delightful manner.

CAMP SHLEIMUS PROVIDES AN ALL-AROUND WHOLE-some summer camp experience. In addition, Rabbi Daniel Mittleman, the camp's learning director, has devised many exciting and innovative programs, which create a spirit of enthusiasm that encourages the children to learn to their maximum potential during the summer months.

The highlight of the project is the Learn and Earn Program,

where boys are able to earn points through their learning. Every time a boy comes on time to learning groups and pays attention, his rebbi hands him a ticket. On Shabbos afternoons, when boys normally wile away the long hours playing games, the children are invited to participate in a three-hour learning session in the *beis midrash,* which provides another opportunity to earn the coveted tickets.

Even though it is generally difficult to sit and learn during the summer, the boys in Camp Shleimus don't just learn; they learn with excitement and enthusiasm. They run to learning groups, and participate in many of the extracurricular programs, as well. In fact, nearly half of the campers earn the maximum amount of points. This enables them to redeem their well-earned tickets for the highest level of prizes: items worth between $200 and $400, and sometimes more. The prizes include sets of *sefarim* and electronic devices.

Additionally, at the end of each half of the summer, there is a special Learn and Earn barbecue for those who have earned the maximum amount of points. At this exclusive barbecue, the boys who earned these points are treated to steak, as they are recognized and awarded for their efforts.

Because of the complexity of the program, it is imperative that every boy hold onto all of his tickets. The children are warned repeatedly not to lose their tickets. For even after all of their effort, without tickets, there is no prize.

This past summer, Rabbi Mittleman was very excited that his 10-year-old son, Avi, was participating in the program for the first time. That such a young boy was able to learn for three hours on Shabbos afternoon is truly remarkable. Even though Rabbi Mittleman takes great pride in running the program, his son's participation gave him extra satisfaction.

One Sunday morning, Mrs. Penina Mittleman was having a discussion with her daughter Yocheved, who, although she had been dating for over a year, had not yet found the right one. She was well aware that at the age of 21, she was nowhere near spinster-hood. Nevertheless, since each of her older sisters had found her Mr. Right fairly quickly, Yocheved was very frustrated, especially since for the past few months, no suggestions had been forthcoming. As she vented to her mother, Yocheved became very emotional about her plight.

In the middle of their conversation, Avi walked into the bungalow and saw his mother doing the laundry. He had placed his tickets inside his shirt pocket that Shabbos and now, as his mother was emptying the washing machine, he realized that he had forgotten to take the tickets out. Avi knew the rule about keeping your tickets, and it him now that he would no longer be able to participate in the program.

As would be the case with most 10-year-old boys, Avi burst out into tears. "What am I going to do? I don't have any more tickets. Now I won't be able to win the prizes. I can't believe it."

For a child who had persevered in a three-hour Shabbos afternoon learning session, the disappointment of those lost tickets was too much to bear. He continued to cry and shared his frustration with his mother.

Suddenly, Yocheved, who was in the middle of bemoaning her own predicament, turned to Avi and exclaimed, "Why are you crying? Don't you get it? Your father runs the program. He is the one in charge. He will replace your tickets."

Seconds later, Mrs. Mittleman turned to her daughter with a smile. In a slow and deliberate tone, she delivered a most powerful message. "That's right. Why are *you* crying? Don't *you* get it? Your Father runs the program!"

Now the two of them smiled. They realized that the One Who runs the program can do anything. There is no reason to cry.

Three short weeks later, Yocheved got engaged.

Quite the prize.

In the words of Rabbi Mittleman: "The real point of the story

for me is that there is faith, and then, there is faith with clar-
ity. When one has faith with clarity, Hashem provides."

OUR BODY SHOP

The following personal story took place several months ago.
Although I encountered much frustration and aggravation at
the time, I learned an invaluable lesson, one that should last a
long time.

THE LIGHTS ON THE DASHBOARD OF MY CAR WERE A
cause for concern. The "low tire" light, "service engine
soon" light, and "maintenance required" light were all on.
I have a tendency to ignore these lights until I hear rattling, which
lets me know that I have waited too long. However, since I planned
to drive to New York later that week, it made sense to take care of
the lights before they turned into a real problem.

I decided to bring my car to the dealer. The necessary repairs
would then be covered under my warranty, and the service department would make sure to fix the car properly and professionally.
Or so I thought.

When I called and described the problem to the staff at the
dealership's service center, they made it sound like only minor
repairs were needed. They told me that I could drop the car off at
night, leave the keys in the overnight box, and pick it up the following afternoon. So I arrived at the dealership at 8:30 at night,
parked my Toyota Camry, and dropped the keys as instructed.
With bright lights shining throughout the parking lot, I felt confident that I could leave my car there. My daughter picked me up in

our second car and I went home, satisfied with my decision to take care of the car in this manner.

I was only mildly concerned the next day when I was told that my car wasn't ready, since some parts needed to be ordered. The service department told me that I could pick up a rental car for the day. It seemed odd that parts needed to be ordered, as they had told me earlier that only minor repairs would be necessary.

I came in the following day, eager to get on the road. I dropped off the rental car and paid for the repairs since it turned out that I needed a new tire, which was not covered by the warranty. But as I was about to get into the car, I noticed that the entire front fender was smashed in and the bumper was no longer there. I was shocked — and furious.

I walked into the office and insisted that someone come out and take a look at my car. This was not the car that I had dropped off; it couldn't be. I had given them a car that was in perfect or, well, semi-perfect condition. Certainly the body of the car was in good condition, and they gave me a smashed car in return. I was very upset, and I lodged a complaint with the head of the department.

Of course, the managers insisted that the car must have been damaged before they had received it. I maintained that when I dropped off the car, it was not damaged. They gave me all of their bureaucratic mumbo-jumbo and promised me that they would look into the matter; their security cameras record everything that takes place on their property, and they would get to the bottom of this. But when they took a look at the footage on the cameras, they claimed that they were unable to retrieve any conclusive evidence about when the car had gotten damaged. Obviously, they were much less disappointed than I was. I insisted on looking at the video myself, and I was pretty sure that the evidence was conclusive. But when I found out that my insurance company would cover the body repairs under an uninsured motorist claim, I decided to pay the $250 deductible and get my car back.

I walked away feeling like I was robbed. One thing was for

certain: I was never, ever going to trust that car dealer again. I would never let them touch my car. I gave them an opportunity and they had destroyed my trust. They showed me that they were incapable of acting responsibly — and they lost a customer.

After taking some time to collect my thoughts, I realized that I am no different from the dealer. Every person on This Earth has his personal body shop, where he houses his treasured soul. Each day of our lives, Hashem entrusts us with His most prized possession — a neshamah. Every day, when he comes to pick up His "car," He finds that instead of taking care of it, we have smashed it up and damaged it.

But Hashem does not throw a fit and rant. He doesn't demand and threaten. Rather, He trusts us over and over again. For no matter how many times we have disappointed Him, tomorrow can be a better day. Tomorrow we can live up to His expectations and take care of His prized possession, and not damage it as we did every other time.

Yes, He believes in us. And He knows that we have the ability to give back our neshamos in the same condition that we received them.

This is an incredibly encouraging thought. If only we believed in ourselves as much as He believes in us.

"Rabbah emunasecha — Abundant is Your faithfulness."

THE MACHER

URING THE TIME THAT RAV YITZCHAK ELCHANAN SPEK-
tor served as rav of Kovno, a harsh decree was enacted
by the Russian government; it meant that thousands of
boys would be drafted into the army. The edict spelled doom for
the Jewish young men, whose lives would be in both physical and
spiritual danger. Aside from the typical dangers of war, they would
be surrounded at all times by individuals from the lowest rungs of
society. At best, they could remain loners and stay out of harm's
way, but there would be no opportunity for them to eat kosher
food or to perform any mitzvos.

Donning *tzitzis* or *tefillin* in the presence of their hateful non-
Jewish comrades would bring derision, scorn, or beatings. Fur-
thermore, there was no place to obtain any articles needed for
the performance of mitzvos. Where would one obtain a *lulav* and
esrog? Matzah? A shofar? These obstacles were too formidable to
be overcome by a lone Jewish soldier in the middle of a battlefield.

When the day arrived and the dreaded envelope came in the
mail, informing the young men that they were to report to the
nearest army office, families were fearful and broken beyond measure. They tried everything within their power to gain exemption,
hoping they could find someone who yielded some influence in
the government.

When all options had been exhausted, there was still one
avenue: bribing the officials. The families gave either their own
money, or they raised as much money as they could. But after
raising money for a number of young men in the community, it
became more and more difficult to collect the funds. The townspeople were running out of money. Even when they managed to

raise sufficient funds, there was always the delicate task of handing over the bribe. If handled incorrectly, bribing an officer could result in imprisonment or death.

Rav Yitzchak Elchanan was once approached by the father of a young man who had been drafted. He wanted the rav to arrange for someone to act as a go-between, someone who would know how to give over the money to obtain the boy's exemption, without getting anyone in trouble. Rav Yitzchak Elchanan assured the man that he would take care of the matter immediately.

Sure enough, a few days later, the boy was granted an exemption. Grateful that the matter was taken care of in such an expeditious manner, the father returned to Rav Yitzchak Elchanan to thank him for his involvement. After expressing his appreciation, he asked the rav who had acted as messenger. But the rav would not reveal who his *"macher"* was, though he maintained that the *macher* he had used was the best in the business. The father persisted and asked the rav to reveal the intermediary's name, so that others could benefit from his services.

With a wry smile, the rav agreed, and he related the following:

> When you asked me to find someone to deliver the bribe, I really didn't have anyone to carry out the mission. However, a few minutes earlier, a poor, orphaned girl had come to me, crying bitterly about her hopeless situation. She desperately wanted to build her own home. Yet without a dowry, there was no way anyone would marry her.
>
> When you came into my house and handed me a large sum of money to be given to the appropriate intermediary, I took the money and agreed to do as you asked. Then I lifted my eyes toward Heaven, and I cried out, "Ribbono Shel Olam, I can either send this money to a non-Jewish politician, or I can give it to this broken daughter of Yours."
>
> I decided to give the money to the young woman, and I asked her to pray on your son's behalf. I believed that the

Al-mighty, the Father of all orphans, would listen to her cries and her prayers, and get your son an exemption.

She was obviously successful in nullifying the decree and saving your son from a dreadful fate.

The father listened incredulously; this was definitely not the *macher* he had had in mind. Nevertheless, he thanked the rav for all his efforts and began to walk out of his house. Suddenly, he stopped. He smiled at the rav and asked, "Did the orphan girl have someone specific in mind when she said she wanted to get married?"

The rav understood the implications of the question. Within a few weeks, the young girl's dream was realized; she had found her match. Not only had she saved the young man for whom she had prayed, but she had found in that very same young man her husband.

The *Macher* made it happen. He always does.

KEEPING IT TOGETHER

ONE NIGHT IN THE KRAKOW GHETTO, MOSHE SHEINFELD and a group of his friends decided to break the 7 o'clock curfew and risk their lives to learn in the *shtiebel*. Although they had to learn without even lighting a candle, and needed to be very quiet, they felt it was worth it. They gained inspiration and strength just by being there; it brought forth memories of the time before the Nazis invaded their lives, when they had spent most of their days and nights within the *shtiebel's* hallowed walls.

The building was four stories high. They holed themselves up in a large room at the end of the hall on the fourth floor. On this particular night, there were over 30 young men in the room, and the learning was intense. For a few hours, they were able to forget about the horrors they had lived through, and were still living through. Suddenly, right before midnight, there was a loud banging on the door of the building. The Nazi guards had found them!

The guards began climbing the stairs, their screams accompanied by the incessant barking of the dogs. The boys knew that the end was near. They wanted to run and hide but there was nowhere to go. Yankel Gefen, the leader of the group, was not yet 20 years old. Without saying a word, he managed to convey the importance of remaining silent no matter what. Still, each boy's heartbeat sounded to him like a drumbeat.

Each approaching step of the Nazis was accompanied by their wild and unnecessary gunfire, shattering the silence in the building. They were coming closer and closer, and there was nothing that the boys could do. Their faces went white with fear, yet no one moved.

All of a sudden, one of the boys could no longer control himself and screamed out, "They're here!"

The other *bachurim* were terrified, realizing that the scream may have expedited their capture. But Yankel Gefen walked up to the boy with sure steps and instructed him not to make another sound. Yankel stood right next to him, just to make sure that he would not give away their location with any additional outbursts.

The shouting and barking increased. The Nazis were now on the third floor and the clock was ticking away.

And then, it was almost quiet again.

The boys heard the guards march down the steps as the barking diminished. For some reason, the soldiers had decided that there was no reason to go up to the fourth floor. As hard as it was to believe, the young men were saved.

They peeked out the window just to make sure, and saw the soldiers leaving, together with their dogs. The boys wanted to jump up and scream and sing and dance, but they had to be content with merely feeling a sense of relief, and a very strong sense of gratitude to Hashem that they had survived.

After they were certain that the danger had passed, Yankel approached the boy who had screamed. He looked at him intently and remarked, "*Di hust zich farloiren* — You lost yourself. It is true that they were here, as you said. But you were telling us something we all knew; we all heard the screaming, the barking, and the shooting. And the *Aibeshter* was also here. When you let out that scream, you showed a lack of faith in Hashem's ability to save us.

"The *pasuk* [*Yirmiyah* 17:7] says, '*Baruch hagever asher yivtach baShem* — Blessed is the man who trusts in Hashem.' There is a special blessing for one who puts his faith in the Al-mighty." Yankel also spoke to the rest of the boys about the responsibility we have to believe in the Al-mighty at all times, and to place our trust in Him.

For over an hour, with the world in unprecedented chaos, Yankel Gefen, a 19-year-old boy who carried the world on his shoulders, spoke about the importance of staying calm and unruffled at all times.

This idea does not apply only to those who are holed up in an abandoned shtiebel, petrified that their wildly beating hearts will reveal their hiding place. It applies to each and every person, regardless of the particular challenge he is going through. If one remains composed and even keeled, that, more than anything else, shows how much he truly believes.

If we could maintain our equilibrium at all times, the difficulties we face would be so much easier to bear.

THE GAMES WE PLAY

*An elderly gentleman had a question for the Chofetz Chaim:
"Who will be judging me when I move on to the Next World?"*

*The Chofetz Chaim assured the fellow that he still had time
before he died. Then he answered his question. "After a person
leaves this world, he is judged by the giants of his generation."*

*The fellow smiled and said, "Well then, Rebbi, since you
are the giant of our generation, would you be able to judge me
now and tell me what my destiny will be?"*

*The Chofetz Chaim dismissed the notion that he was one
of the giants of the generation. However, he stressed that the
Heavenly judgment is very strict, and that the sinners will be
ashamed of all the sins they committed.*

*Then he shared a story that portrays the shame a person
will feel when he is judged by Hashem.*

*By way of introduction, the Chofetz Chaim explained that
approximately 200 years before his time, there was a maggid
from Vilna named Rav Feivel. He traveled all over and spoke
to large crowds. Many hundreds of people came to hear him
speak. On one occasion, these were his words:*

"WHEN WE WERE CHILDREN, WE LEARNED IN A one-room *cheder*. There were 15 of us and our rebbi's name was Reb Dovid. When he taught us, we listened attentively and our eyes were glued to his every move. We learned diligently and utilized every moment that he was in the room. But on occasion, for no apparent reason, he would leave. He must have had some personal business to attend to. As soon as he left, the quiet and order went with him, and the atmosphere in the room turned completely chaotic."

Sitting in the audience were a number of Rav Feivel's childhood friends. He looked out into the crowd and called out to them, "Do you remember the games we used to play? We played a game called Army. The strongest boy in the room appointed himself as the monarch and ruler of the classroom, while other boys assumed the subordinate roles. There were generals, lieutenants, and captains.

"Reb Zanvel, do you remember the game?" The elderly gentleman sitting in the front row nodded and smiled as he clearly recalled the transformation that took place when his rebbi left the room.

"Of course, the twins," continued Rav Feivel, "Elisha and Yonah, were the unfortunate recipients of some of the punishments administered by the governing army." The two brothers, now surrounded by scores of grandchildren, nodded in amusement. They remembered the scene. Although they suffered some bruises from those ordeals, 70 years later it was comical to think about the boys' antics.

Rav Feivel continued to describe the scene in detail, explaining that only a few of the boys managed to remain seated. In spite of everything that was going on around them, they seemed to have an awareness that the rebbi would not be gone for long. In fact, he would appear quite suddenly.

"With one twist of the door handle," went on Rav Feivel, "the rebbi was standing before us. Everyone stopped what he was doing immediately. In a matter of seconds, all the boys scurried back to their seats around the table. The monarch was no longer the ruler. The governors were no longer governors. The generals were no longer generals, and the guards were no longer guards. The soldiers put away their sticks, and those who were beaten picked themselves up off the floor. Within a moment or two, we went back to learning just as we had before he left.

"The rebbi rewarded those who had behaved even while he was gone, while those who had instigated or gone along with the trouble were ashamed of their wild behavior." By this time, every set of eyes in the room was riveted on Rav Feivel and his intriguing anecdote. The maggid saw that most of the people in the audience couldn't help but smile as they thought of the children who were caught red-handed when the rebbi returned to the classroom.

Without warning, the maggid banged on the *bimah* and cried out, "The *pasuk* in *Malachi* [3:1] tells us, '*U'fisom yavo el heichalo ha'Adon asher atem mevakshim* — Suddenly, the L-rd Whom you seek will come to His Sanctuary.'

"When *HaKadosh Baruch Hu* stood before us, in clear view, we listened to His every word and behaved like angels. But then, He left. Although we know that He will return, now that we are in exile, chaos has ensued. The bullies appoint themselves as rulers over their contemporaries, and the mindless followers administer their pointless punishments to those beneath them. In their foolishness, they fail to realize that it is only a game, that they are no more in charge than anyone else. The vast majority of those in the 'classroom' go along with the game and act with rowdiness and lack of control.

"But *pisom,* suddenly, everything will change. With one twist of the door handle, and one swing of the door on its hinges, the game will be over. The governors, generals, lieutenants, and soldiers will all go back to their places. The beaten and oppressed will dust themselves off and laugh at the instant shame of their oppressors.

"And only the very few who remained in their seats, well-behaved and attentive, only they will merit the reward from our *Melamed* [Teacher]."

Rav Feivel looked at the now serious crowd. "Yes, one day soon, with a turn of the door handle, Eliyahu HaNavi will suddenly appear and herald the coming of Mashiach and the dawn of Redemption. When Hashem appears, those who behaved while He was gone will be rewarded. The rest will be embarrassed and ashamed about how they acted."

It won't be long before Mashiach suddenly arrives. Let us make sure we are ready, and on our best behavior.

THE BEST SEGULAH OF ALL

We live in a world of quick fixes, in a society in which we want everything done immediately. This is the era of the microwave ovens, instant emails, and text messaging. It's hard to fathom that it used to take months for a letter to arrive from across the world. Nowadays, if it takes more than a few seconds, we become aggravated, agitated, and annoyed. Yes, it is the "in by 9, out by 5" world.

When it comes to our prayers, however, we fail to understand that it does not work that way. When something is meaningful, we must spend time and effort on it.

This brings us to the topic of segulos (spiritual remedies) and kemeyos (amulets). While there is no doubting a tzaddik's ability to bring about healing and salvation through amulets or spiritual remedies, nothing can take the place of pure, unadulterated faith. When we believe, truly believe, that the Al-mighty can bring about our salvation, then we have a mightier tool than any possible segulah.

RAV YAAKOV MUTZAFI, WHO WAS ORIGINALLY FROM Baghdad, eventually became a *maggid shiur* in the She-mesh Tzadkah shul, as well as the head of the Sephardic Eidah HaChareidit of Jerusalem. He often lectured on the importance of trusting the *Ribbono Shel Olam*, while spurning the belief in miraculous recoveries.

He would cite Chacham Mordechai Sasson, one of the Sephardic sages of Baghdad, who was known to bring about salvations through amulets. However, Rav Yaakov insisted that the salvation had nothing to do with Chacham Mordechai and nothing to do with the amulets. Rather, it came through the individual's faith in the Al-mighty. He was asked, "If that is the case, then why use them at all?" To which he replied, "The only reason we have the amulets is so that the miracles will not be considered open miracles."

To prove his point, he told over an enlightening story.

A couple had a problem. Their baby cried incessantly, day and night. No matter what his parents tried, he did not stop screaming. Desperate for a solution, the parents turned to the traditional doctors and solicited advice from the experts. The specialists ran all types of tests, yet they could find nothing wrong with the child. Nobody had any idea why he would not stop screaming.

His parents' frustration mounted and their patience waned. They could not eat or sleep; they didn't have a moment of relaxation. Day after day, week after week. But perhaps what bothered them most was the fact that their child was suffering. Emotionally torn, they felt guilty that sometimes, as the incessant cries grated on their nerves, their compassion turned to anger.

One day, his mother took him for a walk. She figured that if she could get some fresh air, she would have a bit more patience. While she was out, she walked to the marketplace to buy some items that she needed for the house. On the street, she noticed a page torn out of a Chumash. She bent down and picked it up. She kissed it and cleaned it off, and then she said to herself, "Perhaps the Al-mighty is sending me a special gift.

Maybe this holy page will bring my child a recovery and get him to stop crying."

When she arrived home, she placed the piece of paper very carefully on the table. With tears in her eyes, she prayed intensely, from the depths of her heart. "Ribbono Shel Olam, Master of the World, I am a simple woman who does not even know how to read the words of Your holy books. But I do know that the paper that I picked up comes from Your holy Torah. Please, I beg of You, allow this to serve as a healing amulet, and bring my child some peace and serenity."

She rolled up the piece of paper and placed it inside a tiny vial. She attached it to a piece of string, and tied it around her screaming child's neck. Within moments, her child closed his eyes and drifted off to sleep.

From that moment on, his behavior changed drastically. His crying stopped and his demeanor was completely transformed. A smile appeared on his cherubic face. For the first time in months, his mother smiled, as well.

When the boy's father came home, he immediately noticed the sense of calm and quiet that filled the home. Unable to control his smile, he looked at his wife and wondered aloud what type of miraculous recovery had transpired. She told him the story of her "amulet" and her accompanying prayers.

Then she said, "Look at the power of our holy Torah. This is what brought about our child's salvation."

However, when he opened the amulet and looked at the page she had inserted, her husband began to tremble. "What have you done? This is a page from the Tochachah, in which the greatest of curses and fiercest of warnings are given to the Jewish people! On the page that you inserted [Devarim 28], it is written that the Al-mighty will smite His people with insanity. Further on, it says that in the morning, they will say, 'Who can give back last night!' And in the evening they will say, 'Who can give back this morning!' This is the exact opposite *of what we need. This has been our problem. Our nights have turned into days, and our days into nights. And we are going out of our minds with anger and frustration!"*

His wife turned pale, but then she defended herself. "How should I have known what was written? All I knew was that this was a page from the Torah. I placed my trust in it, and I prayed from the depths of my soul that in its merit and in the merit of the holy words that are written on it, the Al-mighty should send a complete recovery to my child. And look! Look at what happened. He sent a miraculous recovery!"

Rav Mutzafi concluded his story and exclaimed, "That is the power and strength of complete faith. It can transform the most terrifying curses into the most beneficial blessings. It all comes down to what one believes."

GAINS AND LOSSES

We recite the berachah acharonah (after-blessing) of Borei Nefashos many times each day. The words, though, are somewhat perplexing. We mention that the Al-mighty is a "Borei nefashos rabbos ve'chesronan — One Who creates numerous living things with their deficiencies" (see Rashba: Shailos U'Teshuvos I:149).

Hashem could have created us without the need to eat, but we thank Him for creating us with our lacks and deficiencies. To illustrate this point, Rav Avrohom Ganochofsky told the following story.

AFTER ENDURING THE HORRORS OF THE HOLOCAUST — he had lost his wife, children, and all relatives and friends — Heshy Blassman finally made his way to America. As soon as he arrived, he began looking for a job, which proved to be another challenge. He didn't speak the language and had no skills to speak of. He asked around but wherever he went, the response was the same: "Learn the language, and then we will see what we can do for you." Heshy's frustration grew by the day, until someone told him that the local synagogue was looking for a *shammas* (sexton). *Finally, something I can do*, he said to himself.

The meeting with the shul's board members went well. He was able to answer all of their questions to their satisfaction — until they asked him if he spoke English. When he answered in the negative, they apologized and said that they could not hire him. He was devastated; he couldn't understand why English was a prerequisite for the job.

The board members explained that at times, irreligious people come to the synagogue for a *simchah,* and they either need someone to show them the place and tell them the page number in the *siddur,* or they need to ask directions when they are ready to leave the shul. Therefore, the *shammas* must know how to communicate with these guests in English. Heshy pleaded with the board members, but to no avail. If he didn't know English, they would have to look for someone else.

Left with no choice, Heshy borrowed money from an acquaintance, and set up a pushcart on a streetcorner. If he owned his own business, he reasoned, he could speak any language he wanted. He bought some household items and began to sell them. Before long, he paid back the money he had borrowed, and began to save up for another pushcart.

His business began to flourish. After a few years, he had enough money to open a storefront. That store proved successful, and he opened another, and then another. After a while, Heshy began to buy factories, as well. Eventually, he had hundreds of employees in his company and became a millionaire.

One time, a merger with another company was proposed. Heshy, who had developed a keen business sense, believed that this was a worthwhile opportunity. He met with the top executives of the other company, and they were extremely impressed with him as a person. After a few months, they decided to go ahead with the merger, as they were confident that it would be a profitable venture. A meeting was set up for the following week to work out all the details.

Along with his trusted assistants, Heshy came to the high-rise Manhattan office building. The other group also arrived with their lawyers, and the two interested parties met in the boardroom, which boasted a polished mahogany table and well-upholstered chairs. The expensive lighting and plush carpeting completed the effect.

The papers were placed on the table. Though Heshy was sitting right next to his lawyer, his future partner wanted him to look over some of the papers, as well. But Heshy told the man that the papers were of no use to him, explaining, "I don't read English."

A hushed silence fell over the room. Everyone stopped what he was doing, as all eyes turned toward Heshy. With a broad smile, he quipped, "If I became a millionaire without knowing English, what would I have become had I known English? I would have become a *shammas* in a synagogue."

Then, as they listened in amazement, he proceeded to tell them his story. It was only because he was unable to speak the language that he was forced to look for a way to earn money despite the language barrier. And that was how his business began.

Many times, when things don't work out the way we expect, our disappointment weighs us down. It is hard not to think of the "what if" scenarios.

Yet very often, those setbacks, those chesronos (deficiencies), turn out to be our greatest blessings.

To Light Up
The Darkness

ON JULY 24, 1982, PHANTOM PILOT GIL FOGEL WAS FLY-
ing over Lebanon, along with Major Aharon Katz, when
their plane was shot down by a Syrian missile. As the
plane descended, Gil ejected himself from the plane. Major Katz
was killed in the incident, while Gil was discovered by Syrian
forces and taken into captivity.

Nearly a year and a half later, Gil lay in his cell, wondering if he
would ever see his loved ones again. For all he knew, they assumed
he was dead and would never look for him. There had been Israeli
soldiers who were shot down and never heard from again. Perhaps
he would be one of those. He could not help but wonder how his
family was doing. Did they think of him often? In truth, the Israelis
were working on a plan to swap him for other prisoners, but he
knew nothing of this.

While still in training, Gil had been taught that it is imperative
for POW's to keep track of the days of the week and the months.
This gives a prisoner a sense of order and helps him maintain
some semblance of normalcy. Thus, one of the first things he had
done in prison was get hold of a calendar. Hence, he was able to
follow the seasons and the Yamim Tovim.

Still, Gil could not help but grow despondent. But then, a
few weeks before Chanukah, he thought of an idea. If the guards
discovered what he was doing, he knew he would be punished
severely. Yet he needed it; he needed to somehow bring some light
into his dark existence. He needed to feel the Presence of the Al-
mighty in the hopelessness of his prison cell.

Although most of the guards were far from friendly, a few

had a modicum of decency. It was from those few that he would obtain some of his most basic needs. First, he managed to procure a tube of toothpaste. Instead of using it to brush his teeth, he cut it into eight separate parts, which he formed into receptacles. After that, he tore some threads from his blanket and rolled them into wicks.

Every morning he would receive a meal. It wasn't anything to speak of, just something to help him live from day to day. He would extract some of the oil from the food and save it in the round receptacles he had fashioned out of the toothpaste tube.

After a few weeks of planning, he had almost everything he needed. He had a menorah, wicks, and oil. But he still didn't know how he would get a light. As the days passed, he began to wonder if his plan would come to fruition.

From time to time, his captors would take him from his dark and decrepit prison cell, clean him up, and place him in front of the international authorities. They wanted to show the world that they took good care of their prisoners. On the day before Chanukah, the guards barged into his cell to prepare him for another "performance." He had lost a lot of weight since he was captured, and he looked frail and gaunt. They handed him new clothing and tried to put some color in his cheeks.

All this time, his mind was elsewhere; he was desperately trying to find a light. He had put so much effort into making his menorah, and he hoped that his plan would not fail now. As he sat in the Syrian official's office, waiting to meet with the International Red Cross, he looked down at his feet, and he could hardly control his excitement. There were eight matches right there on the floor! Clearly, this was a message from Hashem, a gift to ignite a spark in his soul, to give him hope in his captivity.

He waited until no one was looking. Then he bent down, picked up the matches, and hid them in his sock. When the representatives of the Red Cross met with him, they seemed pleased with his condition. Little did they know that his good spirits had nothing to do with the way the Syrians were treating him, but were only because he had found a treasure.

The next evening, darkness settled in on Damascus. Every other evening, the setting sun signaled another miserable night of crushing loneliness. But tonight was Chanukah.

Gil took out his makeshift menorah, which looked more like an arts-and-crafts project made by a 5-year-old than a full-fledged menorah. To Gil, though, it was the most beautiful menorah he had ever set his eyes upon. He removed the first match, struck it against the wall, made a *berachah,* and lit the wick.

Gil could not help but think of his family. Tears streamed down his cheeks as he sang *Maoz Tzur* and all the other Chanukah songs he knew. At the same time, the irony of the whole situation was not lost on him. On Chanukah, the Jews celebrate their triumph over the Syrian-Greek forces. Tonight, in his own little way, in a dark and dank cell in Damascus, Syria, he, too, was victorious.

On June 28th, 1984, Gil Fogel, along with five other prisoners, was granted freedom in exchange for Syrian prisoners. Additionally, six dead bodies of Israeli soldiers were released, among them Major Aharon Katz.

Gil had to wait a number of years before he was able to relive his harrowing experiences in the Syrian prison and document them. When he did, he made sure to write about the one night in which he experienced light, the one night that gave him hope.

THE PIECES
OF THE PUZZLE

*Like many other tzaddikim of yesteryear, the Vilna Gaon, Rav
Eliyahu Kramer, would often go into self-imposed exile. He
would travel from town to town, never staying in one place for
any length of time. Perhaps in so doing, he identified with the
pain of the Divine Presence, which is in exile since the destruction of the Beis HaMikdash. During his travels, he kept his
identity a secret, never revealing his greatness.*

*Though the Vilna Gaon, also known as the Gra, spent his
days immersed in Torah study even while traveling, he made
it a point to cull lessons from his surroundings and his inter-
actions. The following story, which took place during one of
those exiles, was told by the Gra himself.*

A FTER STAYING AT ONE HOME FOR SEVERAL WEEKS,
the Gaon decided that it was time to move on. The
people who had hosted him were very fine people, and
their hospitality was exemplary. Although they had a very modest
home, when it came to the mitzvah of *hachnasas orchim* (welcoming guests) they spared no expense.

They had no idea who the Gaon was, yet they sensed that he
was no ordinary wayfarer; there was something special about him.
He spent all his time learning, and there was an air of holiness that
seemed to envelop him. Thus, when he told his host that he was
ready to depart, the man approached him and said, "I don't know
who you are, but I can see that you are a holy person. I was wondering if I could ask you for a favor. Since you just stayed in our

home for a few weeks, would you be able to tell us if there's any area in our household that can use some improvement? If there is, we would be very grateful if you could let us know, as we try to live our lives according to the dictates of the Torah."

The Gaon had not come to give *mussar*. But once the fellow had asked, he decided to share something he had noticed. "Chazal [*Yevamos 62b*] say that a man who does the following will merit harmony in his marriage: '*Ha'oheiv es ishto ke'gufo ve'hamechabdah yoser mi'gufo* — One who loves his wife like he loves himself, yet honors her more than he honors himself,' for example, by buying her nice clothing and jewelry. I noticed that every morning you make a cup of coffee for your wife, while you don't make one for yourself. I know that money is tight, and I presume you don't have enough money for two cups of coffee. But if that's the case, you should split a cup with your wife. Why do you give her more than you give yourself? How does that fall into the category of loving her like you love yourself?"

The fellow thanked his guest for his suggestion and explained, "After you hear my story, you will understand why I give my wife the coffee instead of sharing it with her or keeping it for myself."

As a young boy, I was extremely bright and I learned with great diligence. The people in my hometown took note of my talents. As such, when I was only 12 years old, one of the wealthiest people in the city approached my father and offered me his daughter's hand in marriage. My father, who was the town's rabbi and a very poor man, felt that this was an opportunity that was too good to miss. He was thrilled at the prospect of having someone take care of me for the rest of my life.

The terms of my engagement were as follows: I would learn for the next six years under a private rebbi hired by my father-in-law, who would help me maximize my potential. When I turned 18, I would marry the wealthy man's daughter, who would be furnished with an expensive trousseau and

*large dowry. In addition, my father-in-law would support us
after our marriage, so I could continue to learn undisturbed
— indefinitely. The terms were written up in a contract, both
sides signed, and we got engaged.*

*The next six years were wonderful. I was able to learn
undistracted and reach great heights, while my parents were
thrilled that I did not have to struggle; I was well fed and
slept on a regular bed with a mattress. Then, right before my
18th birthday, just a few weeks before the wedding, calamity
struck. My future father-in-law's ships, which were all at sea,
capsized in a horrendous storm. He was left penniless.*

*My future father-in-law could barely feed his family at
home, let alone provide his daughter with a handsome dowry.
He certainly wasn't going to be able to take care of me for the
rest of my life. Thus, with a heavy heart, my father called off
the wedding.*

*The broken engagement caused my future wife and her
whole family great embarrassment. One day they were on top
of the world, and the next day they were penniless. They had
no choice but to leave the city and try to restart their lives
somewhere else.*

*In the meantime, other wealthy people in the town were
eager to offer their daughters to me. Another one of the rich-
est men in the city, a well-respected man who supported many
institutions, approached my father and offered similar terms.
He, too, promised that I would be able to sit and learn for as
long as I liked. Within a few weeks, we were married. It was a
lavish wedding, attended by many distinguished people.*

*Our marriage was going well, and we didn't have any wor-
ries. Everything was absolutely perfect and blissful.*

Then suddenly, everything changed.

*One morning, I woke up with a few blisters on my skin,
which at first seemed minor. Over the next few days, however,
the sores began to spread. By the time a few weeks had gone*

by, my entire body was covered with oozing lesions. My wife assumed that it was some sort of infection, which would soon pass. However, the doctor I visited believed that my condition was contagious. In fact, he said that my wife and I should not reside in the same house.

Meanwhile, my father-in-law arranged for the best doctors to examine me. The doctors came from all over the region, each spent time examining and diagnosing my skin condition, but no one was able to come up with a solution.

With each passing day, I grew more and more despondent, until one day, my world came crashing down on me. My father-in-law came to visit and informed me that since it appeared that I would never recover from this disease, it would only be prudent and fair on my part if I gave my wife a divorce. I was devastated. I begged him for more time, but he was insistent and left me with no choice. So I gave my wife a divorce. Once more, I was all alone.

The people of the city took pity on me and allowed me to stay in the local hekdesh [hostel]. They provided me with food and drink and gave me creams and ointments to soothe the painful sores all over my body. Days turned into months, which turned into years. And still, I was stricken with this awful skin disorder.

One day, a poor man came from out of town. His downtrodden appearance told me that he, too, had suffered in his lifetime. We told each other our tales of woe, and we shared in each other's misery. After spending a few days with me, the man had a suggestion.

"I know that you are a scholar, but let's face it — your disease is preventing you from marrying a normal girl. I have a daughter who is afflicted with a similar disease. Would you consider marrying her?"

Although I was unhappy with the suggestion, I realized I had very few options. If I wanted a partner in life, I was going to have to settle. And so, I agreed to meet his daughter. I only met the young lady for a few moments, yet I was filled with pity for her and decided to marry her. Who could better understand how she felt than I?

When we married, there was no lavish ceremony and no dowry.

When the wedding was over, I noticed that my new wife was crying bitterly, which made me very sad, as well. At first, she seemed inconsolable. Eventually, I managed to calm her down and got her to tell me why she was crying. This is the pitiful story she told:

"My father was a very wealthy man, and I was engaged to one of the finest, most brilliant scholars in the region, who wanted to learn for the rest of his life. My father was going to support us to make my chassan's dream a reality. But then, one day, my father lost his entire fortune."

As my wife told her story, I began to wonder: It all sounded so familiar. I thought that I knew the ending of the story, but I kept quiet and let her continue.

"After my father lost his money, the chassan's father insisted that since my father was unable to keep his end of the deal, the engagement should be broken. I became depressed and disheartened. Eventually, I developed this skin infection. And now, here I am, married to a pauper, with the same kind of illness."

As she finished speaking, I could not help but smile. My wife could not understand why I was smiling, nor could she understand why I asked her for the name of her original hometown. Nevertheless, she told me the name, and sure enough, it was the same town where I had grown up. However, my wife still had no idea what I was driving at, until I blurted it out.

"I was the young man you were supposed to marry. I was the one who was engaged to you. It was my father who broke the engagement!"

That night, we cried for the pain of the past and dreamt about our dreams for the future. Remarkably, a few short weeks later, both of us were healed from the skin ailments. It was the Al-mighty's way of showing us that we were destined for each other.

Although we thought we could orchestrate things in a different manner, what is Divinely ordained will be. After causing my dear wife much heartache and pain, I learned that lesson the hard way.

The host finished his story and now turned his attention to the question at hand. "My dear guest, you asked me why I make my wife a cup of coffee every day instead of keeping it for myself or sharing it. The answer is: As you have heard, I caused her tremendous grief, heartache, and pain. Thus, I decided that throughout the course of our marriage I would do whatever I could to make it up to her. My small token cup of coffee every day is a reminder of how much I owe her."

When the Gra, the great Rabbeinu Eliyahu of Vilna, told this tale, he added, "My entire self-imposed exile was worth it, if only to hear this story and learn of the incredible Hashgachah Pratis [Divine Providence] it conveys."

All too often, when it comes to shidduchim, we feel that we must dot every "I" and cross every "T." But no matter how much we feel we are in control, the Al-mighty is the One Who runs the world.

If we would let go and just submit ourselves to His will, we may be able to see how He fits every piece into His magnificent puzzle.

KEEPING WARM

Rav Asher Chadad heard this story from his mother while he was still a child, and it made a great impression on him. When he grew older and became a marbitz Torah, he shared this story often, as it was one of his favorites.

YOUNG URI LIVED WITH HIS MOTHER; HIS FATHER HAD died years before. Though he and his mother tried to make it on their own, their life was not easy. They lived day to day and scraped together whatever they needed to survive. His mother, Ahuva, was a frail woman. She wanted to protect her son and provide him with proper nourishment, but she was incapable of taking care of him. Thus, despite his young age, he looked after both himself and his mother by begging for food. Ahuva loved her son dearly and tried to discourage him from going out on the streets, but she really had no choice. On most days, Uri would come home at night with enough food for the two of them, and she was very appreciative of his efforts.

At one point, Uri began to think about his future. He knew that he could not continue this way forever. What would happen if his mother would get sick? How would they pay for medical care or medication? What would happen if he would get sick? Who would provide them with food? To prevent these scenarios from coming to pass, he decided to do something drastic.

Instead of going from door-to-door for petty donations, he planned on asking someone who could provide him with much more. There was a very wealthy man in the city, but no one ever asked him for donations because he was a tightfisted miser. When Ahuva learned of her son's plans, she tried to dissuade him, as she knew that the man would slam the door in his face. Why should he have to endure the shame? However, Uri was a strong-minded boy and his mind was made up. He kissed his mother goodbye and headed toward the miser's home.

The large home was impressive, yet intimidating. When he first approached the imposing structure, Uri was hesitant and almost turned around; but every time he thought of heading back, he remembered their dire straits and his fears for the future. He thought about his unfortunate mother and the crushing poverty in their home. With all those thoughts running through his mind, he concluded that he had no choice. Thus, he knocked on the door and waited.

A minute later, the door was opened. Standing before him was the miser of the city. He looked at Uri, and in an annoyed tone, asked him what he wanted. Uri was nervous and jittery, but he managed to state his request.

"My mother and I live alone. My father died a number of years ago, and we have very little money. Every day, I go out to beg and bring home whatever food I can, but it's not enough. I'm concerned that one day I won't be able to do it anymore. I'm worried that I will be sick or my mother will be sick, and we will have nothing to live on. Please, please, I beg you. Please give us some money."

The coldhearted miser looked at the boy with disdain. Then he laughed and tried to close the door, but Uri managed to stick his foot in to stop the door from closing on him. He repeated his request, but now in an even more determined tone: "Please! I promise I will do anything. Just please give me some money."

Impressed by the young boy's spirit, the miser decided to give him a donation. "All right. I will give you 10 golden coins."

Uri could hardly believe what he was hearing. 10 golden coins? That would last him for months, or maybe years.

But before Uri could get too excited, the miser added a condition. "Wait, not so fast. If you want 10 golden coins, you're going to have to earn them. I have to see that you are strong and resilient, so I am going to put you the test. If you go into the river, and stay there with the water up to your neck, from sunset until sunrise, then I will give you the money."

Uri ran home to tell his mother the good news. However, when he told her the terms and conditions of the deal, she refused to allow him to go through with it. "I know that we need the money, but how can I, as your mother, allow you to risk your life to make some money? We have managed until now and we will continue to manage. But I cannot allow you to do it."

Just as Uri had begged and pleaded with the miser, he now pleaded with his mother. Finally, he told her, "I know you don't want me to do it, but I feel we have no choice."

Realizing that there was little she could do to stop him, she gave him a hug and a kiss and told him to be careful. He ran back to the miser and told him that he accepts the terms of the deal. That evening, in the freezing winter, Uri walked to the edge of the river and slowly made his way into the water, until it reached his neck. The water was so cold that he could hardly breathe. Gasping for air, he thought he would give up within the first few minutes. Yet once he put himself in the right frame of mind and he thought about what was at stake, he settled in for a long and frigid night.

Tormented by feelings of guilt, Ahuva stood on the banks of the river and called out words of encouragement to her son, all the while praying that her child would be all right. As the night wore on and the cold air grew more biting, she found some reeds nearby and made a small fire. She knew that there was no way her son could feel the warmth of the fire, but she felt like she had to do something.

Later on in the evening, the cruel and heartless miser came by to see how his ruthless experiment was coming along. He was impressed to find the child standing in the river; he had never expected him to go through with his end of the deal. When he noticed Ahuva standing at the side of the river, and the small fire she had made, he gave a sarcastic laugh. Then he made a snide remark about how cold he was, and how he had to go inside to warm up, and he disappeared.

The night seemed to last forever. The wind howled and made the water painfully cold. Uri began to lose feeling in his extremities. He kept moving around to fend off hypothermia and keep himself from freezing to death. He sang songs to distract himself and to escape to a place in his mind where it was warmer. His mother kept calling out to him and showering him with the words of reassurance. As she cried for her suffering little boy, the tears she shed froze on her cheeks.

At long last, the night was over. As soon as the first rays of the sun peeked over the mountains, Ahuva called out for Uri to come out of the water. She was ready and prepared with blankets. She had no idea how he had survived, but somehow he had. She brought him back home and he sat at the fire. At first, his teeth were chattering and his entire body had a blueish tinge. She had feared that the experience would make him ill, but he seemed fine.

Later that night, when he was back to himself, Uri made his way once again to the miser's home. He knocked on the door, this time with confidence and great satisfaction; soon, he would have the 10 golden coins the miser had promised. But when the miser answered the door, he pretended that he didn't know the boy. "Good evening. Can I help you?"

Uri tried to hold back his astonishment. "Yes," Uri said, "I am here to pick up my reward." But the miser refused to give Uri a penny. He excused himself by saying, "I told you that you have to stay in the water all night, but I never said you were allowed to have a fire nearby to warm you up."

Uri's face turned beet red. Filled with anger, he lashed out at the miser and told him that the fire had no impact on him surviving the night. Alas, his tirade fell on deaf ears. The miser refused to pay and slammed the door in Uri's face.

Overcome with sadness coupled with rage, Uri headed straight toward the governor's mansion. Though he did not know the governor, he hoped he would have mercy on him. When he arrived at the gates, the guards were surprised to see a young boy coming to ask the governor for help. Yet Uri insisted that he had to see the governor. Perhaps it was the curiosity of it all, but the guards allowed him to enter the grounds. Within a short span of time, he was standing in front of the governor.

As he poured out his story, Uri could sense that the governor had mercy on him. He told him about the wretched poverty he and his mother endured and how they survived by Uri's begging. Then he mentioned his worries and how he had made a deal with the miser, who had reneged on his end of the agreement. The governor knew of the miser's reputation. He didn't like him much either. He summoned the crooked, loathsome bully to come to his palace.

When the miser appeared and noticed Uri waiting in a side room, he realized that the boy had informed on him, and he gave Uri a menacing look. As the miser entered the governor's private chambers, the governor did not hide his displeasure. Without smiling once, he asked the miser to tell his side of the story.

Before the miser finished his story, however, the governor asked him if he would like a cup of tea. Surprised that the governor's mood had suddenly changed, the miser accepted his gracious offer and continued to tell his side of the story.

For some reason, the governor turned on the fire and placed the kettle down a few feet away from the stove. Although the action seemed odd, the miser was not going to comment. After 10 minutes, the governor said, "Let's see if the kettle is hot enough for a cup of tea."

By now, the miser thought that the governor was going insane. Obviously, the kettle was freezing cold; it was nowhere near the fire. How could it possibly be hot? He mentioned this to the governor, and the governor looked at him with a gaze that bore right through him.

"Indeed, you are right. There is no way that a fire that is placed so far away can possibly warm up the kettle. If you want the kettle to get hot, it must be placed directly on top of the fire.

"Now that you get the point, either pay the 10 gold coins to the boy and his mother, or I will throw you in jail."

Rav Asher finished telling this story from his childhood and added, "The human heart is the fire for doing ratzon Hashem [will of G-d]. When we want to improve in our avodas Hashem [service], it is not sufficient to place the mitzvos near our hearts. Rather, in order to fulfill ratzon Hashem, mitzvos must be performed with our hearts, and be done with hislahavus, with enthusiasm and passion. That is the only way to come closer to Hashem."

One day, the Governor, HaKadosh Baruch Hu, will prevent the wicked miser, the Satan, from withholding our rewards and give us the compensation we deserve.

Until then, we must look for ways to stay warm.

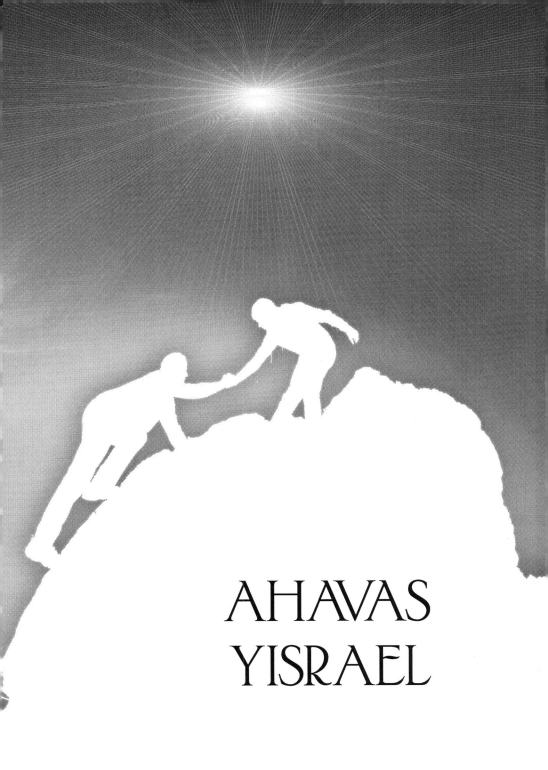

AHAVAS
YISRAEL

A VOICE IN THE WIND

One of the great mashpi'im (men of influence) of the last
generation, Rav Mendel Futerfas, told this tale, which speaks
of the ability of one person to lift another — out of the depths
of despair and the doldrums of misery — and bring him to a
place of hope and possibility.

I N THE LATE 1800'S AND EARLY 1900'S, IF A PLAGUE BROKE
out in Europe or Asia, it could decimate many small villages in
a very short period of time. Nikolayev, a small town in Russia,
had dodged numerous plagues in recent memory. However, when
the disease of typhus broke out in the early 1900's, the village was
not as fortunate as it had been previously. Aside from the devastating physical discomfort and pain that typhus inflicted, there was
additional reason for despair. Anyone who was diagnosed with the
disease was immediately quarantined and sent to a hospital on the
outskirts of the city. No one was allowed to visit these people. They
would languish there for weeks on end, lonely and miserable until
they died a terrible death. Fear mounted throughout the village as
the disease took its toll. It did not make a difference if one was rich
or poor, successful or not. No one was spared.

Not even the rav.

In truth, no one thought it was possible. Rav Meir Shlomo Yanovsky was a gem of a human being. And yet, he too was caught in the clutches of the illness. He was diagnosed by the doctor and immediately taken away to the hospital to be quarantined — and to die.

The townspeople were devastated. They had always turned to their rav for encouragement in times of sorrow. And now, it was their turn to try to find a way to give *him* hope and encouragement. But they knew that the quarantine prevented almost everyone in the town from visiting him. Everyone — except Reb Asher Grossman.

Reb Asher was indefatigable; he never let anything stand in his way, and he certainly wasn't going to let doctor's orders prevent him from visiting Rav Meir Shlomo. Immediately upon hearing the news, he set out toward the hospital. But as soon as he approached, the authorities sent him away. Although he insisted that he was aware of the risks involved and was willing to expose himself to the danger, the doctors would not allow it as they were concerned about the lives of others. Although Reb Asher was less than pleased, he fully understood that he could not endanger others, and so he returned home.

Nevertheless, he knew that he had to do something. So he took his trusted *sefer,* the *Tanya,* and headed once again to the hospital. As before, he was stopped and prevented from entering the building. But this time he had a plan. He asked the authorities the location of the rav's room. When they motioned that it was located on the left side of the building, Reb Asher headed in that direction and opened his *Tanya* to the 11th chapter of the *Iggeres HaKodesh.* Then he stood close to the window of what he thought was the rav's room. Even though he could not be sure that the rav was there, he began to read in a clear, strong voice, *"Ein ra yoreid mi'leMaalah…* — No evil comes down from Above…." He continued to read about how we feel evil or suffering in This World because we don't see things clearly, and how everything is really good. *"Al kein hirchiku middas ha'atzvus be'me'od chachmei ha'emes* — That is why the Kabbalists greatly encouraged people to stay away from the trait of sadness."

As he continued to read, it may have appeared that his voice was trailing off into the distance. In fact, he had no way of knowing if anyone was hearing what he had said. But he was not deterred. The next day, he repeated this practice; he went back to the same place with his *sefer* and once again read aloud, *"Ein ra yoreid mi'leMaalah. . ."* He read until the end of the chapter: "And with this faith, one will merit to see that everything is good."

Reb Asher came back day after day, week after week. He did not know if his friend heard anything he read to him. All he knew was that he was still alive. But he continued to read on. And finally, one day, a miracle happened and the rav was discharged from the hospital and given a clean bill of health.

As soon as the rav was released, word spread among the townspeople of Nikolayev, and the people were filled with joy and gratitude that their rav had recovered. People began to come to his house and visit him. Sure enough, among the very first to arrive was his dear friend, Reb Asher. As soon as the rav set eyes upon him, he walked over to him and embraced him, holding on for a long while. "Reb Asher, you saved my life. Without you, I would never have made it out alive." He cried and held onto his friend as he explained.

"When I was first diagnosed, I was certain that I would succumb to the illness. But as I lay there in bed lamenting my fate, I heard your voice, a gift from Heaven. You didn't even know if I could hear you, but you had faith that somehow the words you were reading would reach my ears — and my heart. You believed in me even when I had lost faith in myself. Your words were like fresh water on a parched soul. Every day that you read to me, I gained strength and became healthier. It was you, Reb Asher, who healed me. It was you who saved my soul."

Reb Asher's eyes filled with tears. He tried to express his great admiration, love, and appreciation but he couldn't speak. He was too overcome with emotion, so grateful to have been given the opportunity to help.

TO SILENCE THE CRIES

RAV AVROHOM GANOCHOFSKY, THE ROSH YESHIVAH OF the Tchebiner Yeshivah, was a *gaon* (genius) and a tremendous *masmid* (diligent student). Every second of every minute of every day was precious to him. Thus, it came as quite a shock to the residents of Yerushalayim to see Rav Avrohom standing on a ladder next to the window of an apartment building, and then later sitting on the ladder's top step, looking into a window of that building.

Mr. and Mrs. Schwartz (not their real name) had gone out for a short while to do some shopping. Their children were asleep, and they did not expect them to wake up any time soon. In their neighborhood, everyone was religious and there was no crime. This provided them with a false sense of security, which made them think they could leave their home unattended for a short while.

Little did they know that shortly after they left, their youngest child would begin to stir. Before long, the whimpers of "Abba. . .. Imma. . ." turned to full-blown screaming. Eventually, his wailing woke all of his siblings. Soon enough, the heartrending cries of all of the children could be heard outside, as well.

Nobody suspected that the children had been left alone; passersby assumed that the children were simply cranky. Instead of doing anything about the situation, they continued on their way.

But one individual did not.

Rav Avrohom, who was on his way home from yeshivah, could not help but hear the crying, and the children's cries tugged at his sensitive heart. He realized that these were not the cries of a child to his mother who is right there with him. Still, he could have excused himself and rationalized that there was nothing he could do as the crying was coming from a window that was nearly 15 feet off the ground. But that is not the way Rav Avrohom thought or acted. Instead, he searched for a ladder. He knocked on the doors of a few stores, but nobody was able to help him. Finally, he went all the way to his house and retrieved his own ladder from his *machsan* (storage area).

Ignoring the fact that he was a rosh yeshivah and that no one of his stature would ever be seen holding a ladder in the streets of Yerushalayim, he walked purposefully toward his destination. After opening the ladder and assuring that it was steady, he climbed the steps and peered through the window into the room where the children were crying.

With his beautiful smile, calm demeanor, and sweet disposition, Rav Avrohom spoke to the children to alleviate their fears. When they peeked out the window, he reached out to them and handed each of them a candy from his rebbetzin. Almost immediately, the children stopped crying and happily took the candies from his hand. Although wrought-iron bars separated him from the children, he brought a smile to their faces. Their breathing slowly became less labored and they calmed down, as he proceeded to tell them a story. The children stared out the window at their new friend and listened intently to his wonderful tale.

Well into the recounting of the narrative, Mr. and Mrs. Schwartz arrived and immediately realized what had happened. They apologized to their children and promised never to leave them alone again. Then they thanked Rav Avrohom profusely and begged his forgiveness for having inconvenienced him and wasted his time. Rav Avrohom deflected their praise and dismissed their expressions of gratitude, insisting that he had done nothing. He climbed down the steps of the ladder and waved goodbye to his new friends, assuring them that they could come visit him whenever they wanted.

> *Years later, when a talmid asked Rav Avrohom about this episode, he tried to deny it. But then, someone showed him a picture of him sitting on the ladder outside the apartment building, and he had no choice but to admit that the story had actually taken place. Then, in his inimitable way, he shared a few important lessons from the story.*
>
> *First, there is no limit to how far one must go to silence the cry of a child.*
>
> *Second, sometimes we cry to Hashem in pain and in anguish. Although we are unable to feel Him holding us in His arms, we should be aware that He sits right outside our windows and listens to our cries — and reaches inside to hold our hands.*

THE CELL PHONE SITUATION

THE CHILDREN OF REB MENDEL GOLDENFIELD SAT IN the funeral home, ready to bid a final farewell to their father. The large crowd that had begun to assemble gave testament to the fact that their father had been an exceptional human being, beloved by all who knew him. While the family was discussing who should offer the eulogies, one fellow stepped forward. No one in the family recognized him, but he asked to be allowed to give a eulogy, as well. Since so many dignitaries would be speaking, the children dismissed his request and told him that they could not fit him in. But he kept insisting that he had something to share publicly. He appeared to be an *ehrliche* (upright) person, and seeing how much this meant to him, they told him that he could give the final eulogy.

Many eulogies were given that day, extolling the deceased's Torah scholarship and stellar character traits. He was a beloved family man who had meant so much to so many people. Finally, it was the stranger's turn to speak. The family was a bit on edge, wondering what he was going to say. As he began to speak, they noticed that his voice was trembling. He apologized for being so insistent about speaking, but he repeated that he had something very important to share.

> *The truth is that I met the deceased only once in my life. And that was only for 10 minutes. But those 10 minutes made an incredible impression on me.*
>
> *I learn in a yeshivah with 340 other boys. Twice a week, our rebbi gives a shiur to the whole yeshivah. He is very particular that anyone who is not part of the yeshivah may not be present at the time of the shiur.*
>
> *One day, as the shiur was about to begin, an uninvited guest arrived: the niftar, Reb Mendel. He was informed that anyone who is not part of the yeshivah is not allowed to attend the shiur. But he had heard about the brilliance of the shiur and very much wanted to be able to attend. "Torah hi ve'lilmod ani tzarich — This is Torah and I must learn it"; echoing the sentiment uttered so many centuries ago by Rabbi Yehudah HaNassi [Megillah 28a], he begged for permission to stay. The request was brought to the attention of our rebbi, and he reluctantly allowed the man to remain.*
>
> *The shiur began and all seemed to be forgotten when suddenly, the ringtone of a cell phone sounded throughout the*

room. It was coming from Reb Mendel's area. Anyone who has ever attended our rebbi's shiur knows that such a disturbance is not tolerated. Our rebbi seemed agitated as he glared in the direction of the cell phone noise. Reb Mendel put his hands in his pocket and fumbled with his cell phone, trying to figure out how to shut the ringer. However, he was clearly not very astute in this particular area, and it took him a good 10 seconds to turn off the ringer. The maggid shiur seemed upset about the disgrace the cell phone had caused, but immediately thereafter, he continued the shiur.

Five minutes later, the cell phone shrilled loudly and everyone looked anxiously toward our rebbi to see how he would react. Predictably, he stopped midsentence and declared in a sharp tone, "Kach lo lomdim Torah! This is not the way we learn Torah!" He seemed ready to walk out of the room, but then decided that he would try to continue the shiur one more time.

The crowd was aware that the next disturbance would most certainly bring an end to the shiur. They glared angrily at their uninvited guest, as if to warn him that it better not happen again. But it seemed that the phone had been set to alarm mode, and instead of turning off the alarm each time, he had just been pressing the snooze button, causing it to ring again five minutes later.

And so, five minutes later the phone rang again. This time, nothing was said. The rebbi simply closed his sefer, and to the disappointment of everyone present, walked out of the room.

Chaos erupted. All 340 members of the yeshivah expressed their displeasure and voiced their protest over Reb Mendel's negligence and unacceptable behavior. On their way out of the room, each person made sure to make some kind of cynical comment or grimace in his direction. Reb Mendel felt terrible about what had happened, and was filled with remorse that all the young men would not be learning because of him.

At this point, the young man who was eulogizing stopped, while all those in attendance wondered where all of this was heading. What kind of eulogy was this?

After a long pause, and in a voice filled with emotion, the young man cried out, "*Rabbosai*, I was standing next to Reb Mendel the entire time. You cannot imagine the horrible shame he had to endure. I have never seen or heard anything like it in my life."

Once again, the young man paused as he tried to stop his crying. Finally, he blurted out, "I have something to tell you. It wasn't even his cell phone that kept on ringing. *It was mine!* And I didn't know how to turn it off. All the screaming and yelling that was directed at him should have been directed at me. But in order to save me from shame and disgrace, he acted as if it were his cell phone — and he only pretended to turn it off.

"I feel it is important to tell everyone, in a public setting, that just as he endured the shame publicly, he should be given the honor in the same fashion."

Perhaps what makes the story noteworthy is the fact that this was not a calculated act to help another person. Rather, Reb Mendel had trained himself to save others from embarrassment, even at his own expense.

And so, when the opportunity presented itself, he was ready.

NACHAS NOTES

JIMMY BURTON, A SENIOR AT FAIR LAWN HIGH IN NEW JER-
sey, loved spending his Thursday evenings at the Know
and Grow Koffee Klatch Program, in which 30 to 40 public
school children would get together to discuss various Jewish topics at the local coffee shop, and receive a free drink and a bit of
inspiration. A young couple who had recently moved into the area,
Rabbi and Mrs. Sommerstein, were running the program and the
children really took a liking to them.

Jimmy was inspired by the talks at Koffee Klatch, and, because
of his obvious interest, the Sommersteins tried to encourage him
even more. They once saw him walk into a nonkosher restaurant.
As he was about to bite into a hamburger, Rabbi Sommerstein told
him that from now on, he and his wife would provide Jimmy with
a kosher meal on Thursday nights — if he would like to have one.
Slightly embarrassed that he was eating nonkosher food in front
of them, he happily agreed and thanked them for their generosity.

A number of months went by, and Jimmy became more and
more interested in Yiddishkeit. When the idea of spending a summer in Israel came up, he was extremely excited. Know and Grow
was offering public school children an opportunity to spend a
summer in Israel, where they could learn about their heritage and
their land. But when Jimmy brought up the idea to his parents,
they said that he could go if he wanted, but they would not fund
the trip, which cost several thousand dollars.

Jimmy made inquiries to see how he could come up with the
money without his parents' assistance. One of his friends suggested that he buy ties wholesale and sell them from door to door.
Jimmy thought it was a good idea and ordered the ties. But when
the package of ties was delivered, he saw that they were unattract-

ive and outdated, not the type of ties that people would want to purchase. He tried to sell them anyway and went knocking from door to door, but no one was interested. Jimmy began to lose hope.

Then the Sommersteins gave him an idea. They recommended that he go to Beth Medrash Govoha in Lakewood and put the ties out on a *shtender*. They told him to tape an envelope to the *shtender*, so people could put money inside the envelope after choosing their ties. They also instructed him to write down his story and explain that he was a public school boy who wanted to spend his summer in Israel, to learn more about his heritage and his religion — but that he had to raise the money for the trip on his own.

Jimmy drove down to the yeshivah. As he walked into the building, he was overwhelmed by the sights and sounds; he had never seen the inside of a yeshivah and he was very impressed. He set up his self-serve tie stand and taped up the envelope and story. When he returned a few days later, he was thrilled to discover that people had placed money inside the envelope. It seemed like nobody was interested in the ties, but quite a few people were interested in his story. Aside from putting money in the envelope, they also placed small notes along with their donations. Some wished him good luck, while others jotted down a few lines, telling him how proud they were of his efforts. After a few weeks, he had raised enough money to enroll in the summer program.

Jimmy made his final plans and booked his ticket. As the day of his departure approached, Jimmy looked forward to the trip with great anticipation. His parents, though, felt that he was taking his interest in religion a bit too far. Jimmy was disappointed that they did not share his enthusiasm, but he knew that he could not turn back now.

After Jimmy left, Mr. and Mrs. Burton puttered around the house until nighttime. They both hoped that his trip would go smoothly, though neither of them wanted him to completely change his way of life or become Torah observant. As they passed his empty room, they noticed a large manila envelope on his desk.

Mr. Burton picked it up and looked inside. It was full of hand-written notes, some wishing Jimmy good luck and others apologizing that they could not give him more money, but encouraging him to follow his dream. His father and mother read the notes one by one. As they read, their hearts softened and tears filled their eyes.

Then they came across a note that would change their lives forever. It read, "I wish you were my son."

Jimmy's parents began to cry. They had friends whose children were suffering from substance abuse, while others had blue and pink hair, and still others were gallivanting around third-world countries. Their own child wanted one thing: to discover more about his heritage and his religion.

This note finally brought clarity to their lives. They reached out to their son and encouraged him to pursue his dream. And they followed along. Today, all of the family members are observant Jews.

One message stands out. A fellow learning in Lakewood spent a minute jotting down six words. Those six words altered the course of a family's future.

Amazing what just a bit of thoughtfulness can accomplish.

A VERY SAD REQUEST

One year, before the reading of the Torah on Shavuos, Rav Meir'l Mi'Premishlan told over a compelling story.

REB SHIMSHON VERTHEIMER HAD A CLOSE RELATIONSHIP with the king of Austria. The king once asked him why the Jewish people suffer so much, much more than all the other nations of the world. Reb Shimshon responded that their suffering comes because of jealousy and senseless hatred among fellow Jews. The Second Temple was destroyed because of these sins, and it has not yet been rebuilt because we still have difficulty getting along with one another.

The king listened to the response but felt that it was extreme. Could it be that the Jewish people have suffered for 2,000 years, just because they are jealous of one another? He got angry at Reb Shimshon and demanded that he come up with a better answer within three days. If not, the king threatened to exile all the Jews from the land of Austria.

With a heavy heart, Reb Shimshon left the king's chamber. He knew that he had given the true reason, but he had to find a way to prove it to the king. In a *she'eilas chalom* (a question in a dream), he asked for advice, and the answer came immediately. He was told not to worry. In three days' time, all would turn out well.

The next day, the king went on a hunting expedition in the forest with his high-ranking officers. He spotted a deer in the distance and was prepared to shoot, when the deer began running away. The king chased after the deer. During the course of his pursuit, he somehow lost his way. He tried to find his way back to his fellow huntsmen but the more he searched, the more lost he became. As the hours passed and day slowly turned into night, he looked for a beacon of light to help him find his way out of the forest. He climbed a tall tree, and saw a light shining in a nearby village. He climbed down and immediately headed in the direction of the light, hoping to reach his destination quickly.

As he drew closer to the place, he saw that a river separated him from the small village. He was very cold and utterly exhausted from the harrowing day's events. In his desire to find some warmth and rest, he realized that he would have to cross the river. And so, he removed his crown and royal robe and jumped in. Then he swam across, fighting the waters with his last remaining strength.

When he reached the other side, he emerged from the water, drenched and even colder than before. He walked to the first home where he saw light and knocked on the door, expecting that he would be allowed to enter, but the door was slammed in his face. Obviously, the residents could never have imagined that the bedraggled person on their doorstep was the king of Austria. He went from door to door, hoping that someone would allow him in, but each time the response was the same.

Finally, he knocked on the door of a Jew. He knew that Jews are compassionate, so he was hopeful that this Jewish couple would allow him into their home. Sure enough, they were happy to welcome a desperate and freezing stranger. They offered him a hot meal and a warm change of clothing. When he finished eating, he asked if he could stay the night.

Although the woman of the house was cautious and a bit skeptical, they allowed him to sleep in their home. Her husband reassured her that their guest was harmless, but she was not convinced. She thought that he may be a burglar, and that he would clean them out of any valuables they had.

The next morning, their guest thanked them for allowing him to stay over. Then he asked if they knew of someone who could give him a ride to Vienna. Once again, although the man often traveled into Vienna for his livelihood, his wife warned him not to offer their guest a ride. The guest explained that he did not have the money to pay at the moment. However, when he would arrive at his home, he would be more than happy to pay his host handsomely for his time and effort. In fact, he offered a very large sum of money. Eager to make a nice day's wages, the Jew dismissed his wife's concerns and got ready to travel to Vienna. She was still upset and warned him repeatedly that as soon as he would arrive in Vienna, their guest would jump out of the carriage and he would be left with nothing. But her husband would not hear of it; he was certain that he was right. As is so often the case, he would find out the hard way that his wife's concerns were legitimate.

As soon as they arrived in Vienna, the guest directed his driver toward the royal palace. Soon, the Jew's fears were realized when his passenger jumped from the carriage and ran into the forest. The Jew was left alone, with nothing to show for his efforts. And even worse, he would have to face his wife's scorn and listen to how she was right, yet again.

But those were not his greatest worries. As he was turning his wagon around to head home, guards appeared from different directions and demanded that he come before the king. Wondering what else could possibly go wrong that day, he got out of the carriage and walked toward the palace, where he was brought to a room. A few moments later, the guards escorted him before his royal highness. As he looked at the king, he thought to himself that the fellow looked familiar, but he could not place him.

The king came closer and smiled at the Jewish man. Perhaps if the situation were not so absurd, he may have guessed that it was his guest, but the thought never crossed his mind. Finally, the king removed his robe and took off his crown. The Jew could not believe his eyes. It was his guest! Stunned at the turn of events, he listened as the king offered him anything he wanted in return for his kindness.

What an incredible offer! Anything in the world! He could hardly believe his ears. It was too much to take in at one time. When he did not reply, the king offered him riches and a house, but that was not what the man wanted. His silence indicated that he was not satisfied with those generous offers. The king kept upping the ante, but no matter what he offered, it was not enough. Frustrated that he was not able to give the man a reward, the king asked the man to name his price.

His response would reveal to the king much more than he had asked for.

"You know, dear king, that to support my family, I travel from city to city and I sell trinkets out of my wagon. Recently, another Jew in the area began to do the same, and he is taking away my living. Therefore, I ask you to please forbid him from doing so. That is my request."

The king was taken aback. He could not believe what he was hearing. He had offered the man anything in the world, and all he wanted was to prevent another Jew from being his competitor. How very sad and ridiculous it was.

At that moment, everything the king had heard from Reb Shimshon became clear. He ordered his guards to bring Reb Shimshon to the palace, and he told him the entire story: how he had offered the Jewish man anything in the world for helping him in his time of need, and all the man asked of him was to prevent someone else from taking away some of his business.

"Now I know that what you told me is true," he concluded. "The Jewish Temple has not been rebuilt because even when the king offers them anything in the world, all they ask for is the downfall of their competitors!"

Rav Meir finished telling his tale and added: Before one accepts upon himself the sovereignty of the Al-mighty and proclaims the words of the Aseres HaDibros, "Anochi Hashem Elokecha — I am Hashem your G-d," he must first remove all jealousy and hatred from his heart.

A LONG WAY TO GO

THE VIZHNITZER REBBE, THE TZEMACH TZADDIK, HAD only one daughter, named Sarah. Although she was not his only child, she held a special place in his heart. The Rebbe was known as a *baal bechi*, an emotional person who could easily be brought to tears. Hence, when he discovered that his daughter was sick, he was beside himself and cried incessantly on her behalf. As her condition deteriorated and her chances of recovery diminished, the Tzemach Tzaddik grew more and more concerned.

She was receiving treatment in a hospital that was far away. Hence, the Rebbe received a telegram every morning from the doctors, updating him on the condition of his daughter. He would read the cryptic message and try to decipher how much progress, if any, his daughter had made. All too often, the news was not as he had hoped — but at least it was news. He realized that she was reaching a critical stage in her illness and if she did not begin to improve, then there was little hope that she would survive.

Then one day, he waited in vain for the telegram to arrive. With each passing moment, his worry increased. He could not help but wonder why the telegram had not arrived. Did something happen? Was she all right? Why was there a delay? The minutes turned into hours. By the time midday had arrived, he began to fear that something was seriously wrong. He increased his davening efforts as his son, Rav Baruch'l, who later became known as the Imrei Baruch, tried to calm his father's nerves. He assured him that the telegram would certainly arrive in a few moments and that there was no reason to worry. But 1 o'clock came and there was still no telegram.

Finally, after the Rebbe had waited a few more nerve-racking hours, the telegram arrived. Her condition was indeed improving, and they were hopeful that she would have a complete recovery. There was an audible sigh of relief in the home. The Tzemach Tzaddik disappeared into his private chamber and poured out tears of gratitude to the Al-mighty.

Noticing the tears that were still on his father's face and how the day's events had taken their toll on him, Rav Baruch'l asked him, "Father, if you, a prince of the Al-mighty, worried so much about a delayed telegram, what can be said about the rest of us? How will we ever manage in our times of difficulty? How can we be expected to accept these challenging episodes in our lives?"

With tears streaming down his face, the Rebbe responded, *"Mein ti'ere zin*, my dear son, let me explain to you why I was crying so much today. I was created with many faults. And I've struggled my entire life to overcome my shortcomings and failings. After all of my efforts, I would like to think that I was somewhat successful in moving toward my goal of becoming an *oisge'aberte Yid*, a Jew who has worked on himself. But when it comes to the mitzvah of *'ve'ahavta le'rei'acha kamocha*, loving your fellow Jew as yourself' [*Vayikra* 19:18], I try and try and try. Although I have put tremendous work into improving the love I have for a fellow Yid, this mitzvah has always been difficult for me. Until finally, I began to think that I was beginning to make some headway in this area. I really thought that that my level of *ahavas Yisrael* had improved.

"But today, I saw that I still have such a long way to go.

"You see, when I waited this morning to receive the telegram, I was trembling and so nervous about the welfare of my dear daughter. And then I began to think. Every day, hundreds of *kvitlach*, from all over, are presented to me. And there is one common denominator between them; they are all from people in need. Some come from those who don't have children, while others are from people desperate for money to help sustain and feed their families. Some come from families who have lost parents, and some from parents who have lost their children.

"While I waited for the telegram today, I said to myself, *Why, when I read these kvitlach, am I not as worried and as concerned as I am when I wait for the telegram to find out my daughter's medical condition?* And the answer is, quite simply, because I have not reached the desired level of loving another Yid as much as one loves himself. Unfortunately, I worry more about my daughter than I worry about someone else's daughter.

"When it says *'ve'ahavta le'rei'acha kamocha*,' it means *kamocha mamash*, like you for real. This means that one must love another individual as much as one loves himself. Unfortunately, I failed in this regard. And that is why when you saw me earlier today, when I was still waiting for word from the doctors, I was crying so much.

"Because I have so far to go in my *ahavas Yisrael* for a fellow Yid."

AN UNLIKELY SAVIOR

EVERY YEAR, REB MEIR GRUZMAN DELIVERS AN IN-DEPTH course to 100 officers in the Israeli army. In this course, which lasts one week, he covers various topics pertaining to Judaism. He speaks about the history of the Jewish people and the revelation at Mount Sinai. He then follows the travels of the Jewish nation, the 40 years they spent in the desert, their conquest of Eretz Yisrael, and all the other major events that happened to our nation. He tries to make his classes both informative and inspiring. He also tries very hard to stay on topic because if he won't, there will be no end to the questions, which will cause him to skip over some important aspects of the course.

One year, as he was teaching his students about the era of the prophets, one person raised his hand and asked if there are such people around today. Although Reb Meir really did not want to digress, he mentioned the concept of the 36 hidden *tzaddikim* who uphold the world. The questioner seemed pleased with the answer.

Suddenly, another person's hand went up — just what Reb Meir did not want to happen, because he wanted to cover ground. The fellow who raised his hand was a high-ranking officer in the army. Hesitant to allow the man to speak, but feeling that he had no choice, Reb Meir decided to give the officer a chance to express what was on his mind. He would not be disappointed with the results.

"My name is Barak and I am a lieutenant colonel in the army. I thank you for allowing me to speak. I know that you don't like taking questions, but I believe that what I have to say is important. You were speaking about the pious and sacred individuals who have dotted the landscape of Jewish history. I don't want my fellow officers to think that this is something that existed only in the past, and that we don't have such people today. I have a personal story that proves otherwise."

By now, everyone in the room was listening to his story:

I grew up in Bucharest, Romania. My parents observed very few mitzvos and knew almost nothing about our tradition. Communism had done a good job at eliminating almost all traces of religion.

The first three years of my life were uneventful, and I thrived like all other boys my age. But suddenly, something strange began to happen. Whenever I heard a loud noise — such as glass shattering or a bus driving by our window — I would faint.

My parents didn't know what to do. Aside from the fact that I would fall and often hurt myself as I fainted, the unknown damage caused to my body scared my parents to no end. They tried to protect me; when we traveled by train, they would cover my ears, hoping to prevent the fainting.

They brought me from doctor to doctor, but nobody could figure out what was wrong. After many examinations and tests, the doctors determined that the reason for my condition was unknown. They had no diagnosis to offer, and no treatment to suggest. But this was of little comfort to my parents. I will never forget the look on my mother's face when she walked out of that last doctor's office. She thought that I was too young to understand the implications, but I realized that there was no cure for my fainting spells. Who knew how it would affect my future?

One day, my mother was sharing my plight with one of her good friends, who asked her if she had ever taken me to a tzaddik. My mother had no idea what she was talking about. But her friend, who was also irreligious, insisted that she go to a Rebbe. When my mother hesitated, as she really had no interaction with people who were religious, her friend asked her what she had to lose.

Realizing that she had nowhere else to turn, my mother agreed to go to see the holy tzaddik, the Rebbe of Bohush, Rav Yitzchak Friedman. What doesn't a mother do for her sick child?

We arrived at the Rebbe's house, and we were brought into his inner chamber. My mother poured out her heart as she detailed my medical history. I was struck by the Rebbe's presence; he looked so pure and holy. His eyes were soft and understanding, filled with compassion. His face wore a look of concern and caring.

After listening to my mother's presentation, including the names of all of the doctors who were involved in my case, he felt he had a clear picture of my condition. Suddenly, he asked my mother a seemingly irrelevant question: "Is your son a firstborn?"

Although taken aback by the question, my mother answered in the affirmative. The Rebbe then asked if she had performed the mitzvah of pidyon haben, the redemption ceremony of the firstborn. She replied that she had never even heard of it.

In a clear and understandable manner, he explained exactly how to perform this mitzvah, including the necessity of having a quorum of men present during the ceremony, as well as the participation of a Kohen who receives the coins for the redemption.

*The tzaddik then took my hand in his own and wished
me well. He told me that through this mitzvah, I would merit
a long and healthy life, without any more fainting spells. His
smile will always stay in my mind.*

*The next day we did as we were told, and I never fainted
again. The loudest noise causes me no harm.*

All eyes in the room were focused on Barak as he completed
his riveting account. This was the last place they thought they
would hear a story about such a *tzaddik*.

"After we moved to Israel," continued Barak, "the *tzaddik* did,
as well. He had a *beit midrash* on Rechov Sderot Rothschild 112 in
Tel Aviv. I never missed going to see him every year on Erev Rosh
Hashanah. He would always bless me and my family in the warm-
est way possible."

Barak finished his emotional story, and Reb Meir thanked him
for his participation. Indeed, they had digressed, but it was certainly worth it.

For many years, their paths did not cross. Until one day, Meir
met Barak once more — at the Rebbe's funeral, where thousands
had come to pay their last respects. They lost their father, their
leader, their guide and inspiration. Yes, they were all broken.

Those in attendance may have noticed the Israeli officer in
uniform, sobbing bitterly at the Rebbe's grave, and it may have
seemed strange to some. How did this fellow know the Rebbe of
Bohush?

But Reb Meir knew the story.

The story of a little boy who was granted life by an angel of a
man.

THE WHOLE WORLD IS SINGING

While there are many issues that divide the religious and nonreligious factions in Eretz Yisrael, the observance of Shabbos has always been a point of contention. Organizing public protests, when done with the endorsement of our gedolim, is necessary and effective. However, if there were some way to convey the deepest feelings of our hearts, which include love of Hashem and all our fellow Jews, that would be the most effective method of all.

R AV MOSHE ADLER LIVED IN YERUSHALAYIM. EVERY FRIday night after davening, he would go with his children to an old-age home and infuse the residents with some Shabbos spirit. The elderly people eagerly awaited his visit every week. Upon entering each room, he would sing *"Yismechu Ve'Malchuscha."* Afterward, whoever was able to would follow him into a large room, where they would dance together. Some men were confined to wheelchairs, while others got around with walkers and canes. But they held hands and danced for a short while, as they embraced the holy spirit of Shabbos.

This went on for many years. Then one day, the municipality of Yerushalayim decided to buy the nursing home and demolish it. They planned on building the *Tachanah Merkazit*, Central Bus Station, on that spot. The residents of the nursing home were very sad to relocate, but they were not given a choice.

The noisy, bustling Central Bus Station was a stark contrast to the quiet and peaceful nursing home. Yet Rav Moshe's main reason for concern was the fact that the buses ran on Shabbos. Even the buses that officially stopped running for Shabbos would come into the terminal after sunset and cause *chillul Shabbos*.

Rav Moshe was not a screamer or a yeller, yet he was determined to stage a personal protest. Therefore each week, he would walk over to the place where the nursing home used to stand and he would continue his tradition of singing *"Yismechu Ve'Malchuscha."* He pictured himself going from room to room, his visits culminating in a dance with the elderly. He remembered how their eyes would tear up, and recalled as well as their beautiful smiles and the joy on their faces, which was reflected in his children's faces. Now, in this very same place, the holiness of Shabbos was being desecrated.

A group of rabbanim was chosen to visit the home of Ezer Weizman, who served as the minister of transportation at the time. "He would later become the president of Israel. Each one stood up to convey his pain and frustration, and to protest for the honor of Shabbos. But their well-articulated pleas fell on deaf ears. They were entitled to keep the Shabbos, they were told, but they should do so in their own neighborhoods.

The last one to present his case was Rav Moshe. By that time, the minister had already lost much of his patience, and was anxious to move on to his next meeting. Rav Moshe began to speak in his soft voice. "I remember your father, and his parents, Reb Oizer and Rachel. Reb Oizer grew up in a town in Belarus, called Pinsk. In this town, many years before them, lived a great man by the name of Rav Aharon HaGadol of Karlin. He was better known as Rav Ahrele Karliner. He composed a very special Shabbos song that is sung by thousands of Jews every Friday night. It is called 'Kah Echsof.' "

To the shock of everyone present, he began singing the song in a haunting voice. At first, he sang alone. Soon enough, though, the others joined. Before long, the entire room was filled with the sounds of this song.

As Rav Moshe sang, he closed his eyes, oblivious to his surroundings. He concentrated on one thing: the precious treasure that is Shabbos. He sang the words "*Ve'yiheyu rachamecha misgolelim al am kadshecha* — May Your mercy overflow upon Your holy nation," over and over. When he finally opened his eyes, he saw something he never thought possible: Ezer Weizman was singing the tune together with him, and tears were streaming down his face.

When Rav Moshe finished his song, Mr. Weizman picked up the phone and dialed the number of the head of the bus company. He informed him in no uncertain terms that the buses were never to run again on Shabbos. When the fellow on the other line began to protest, the minister put his foot down firmly, stating that there was no room for discussion.

From that day onward, the buses stopped running on Shabbos.

The next week, Rav Moshe continued his tradition of singing "*Yismechu Ve'malchuscha,*" even though it was now peaceful and quiet at the Central Bus Station.

If you listened very closely, though, you could hear the sound of the sweet old men of Yerushalayim singing along with him.

OF BIRTHDAYS AND BENEVOLENCE

IT WAS THE NIGHT BEFORE EZRA'S BAR MITZVAH, AND PREParations were in full swing. All the children's outfits were in need of last-minute alterations. Suits and skirts had to be picked up from the dry cleaners. Cakes had to be baked, and platters had to be prepared. Of course, the *sheitel* appointment had to be confirmed.

In the meantime, the bar mitzvah boy had to practice his bar mitzvah speech. He had the *p'shetl* (speech) down pat; he just had to go over some of the thank-you's with his father.

Yes, there was much to be done and very little time in which to do it.

Suddenly, one of the older girls piped up, "Mommy, did you send an invitation to Mrs. Yankelewitz?" Upon hearing this, Sarah, the bar mitzvah boy's mother, was disappointed in herself; she had forgotten to invite her childless neighbor from down the block. Mrs. Yankelewitz, who was over 80, had lost her husband a number of years ago. Sarah knew how much the old woman would appreciate an invitation. Unfortunately, it had slipped her mind until now. Instead of letting it go, however, she decided to invite her personally.

Sarah walked over to her neighbor and handed her the invitation. One would never have been able to tell that Mrs. Yankelewitz was such a lonely woman, as she always made a point of greeting people cheerfully. This time was no different. With a wide smile, she said to Sarah, "Thank you so much for inviting me. At my age, it is difficult to get out of the house, but I am very appreciative that you thought of me. It also means so much that you came to deliver the invitation yourself. By the way, tomorrow night is also my birthday."

When she came home, Sarah told her husband that she was going to bake a special birthday cake for Mrs. Yankelewitz's birthday. Her husband knew better than to argue with her. He knew that once his wife's mind was made up, there was no way to convince her otherwise, no matter how busy she was.

That night, Sarah continued to bake for her son's bar mitzvah and made one extra cake for her neighbor. She decided that once she was going to do it, she was going to do it right, so she put the words "Happy Birthday" in pink lettering across the middle of the cake. Although it seemed childish to do this for a woman in her

80's, she knew Mrs. Yankelewitz would be gratified to know that it was baked especially for her.

The next day, even with the myriad items that needed to be crossed off her list, Sarah delivered the birthday cake herself. Mrs. Yankelewitz thanked Sarah for the cake but did not say much else. Sarah was a bit surprised that her neighbor had seemed a little subdued when she thanked her for the cake, but she figured that she probably had something else on her mind.

Still, she left with a satisfying feeling, knowing that she had done an act of kindness during her time of joy.

The night went beautifully. Ezra was very poised as he recited his *p'shetl*. Sarah was beaming and so was her husband. She looked around several times, trying to take note of who was there. She looked out to see if her neighbor had come after all, but she didn't see her.

The event lasted nearly four hours: from the time the first person arrived until the last one left. By the time the family arrived home, it was after 11 p.m. Sarah and her husband were both exhausted, but it was a good type of exhaustion. They were grateful to Hashem for having given them such a lovely *simchah*. They understood very well that so many things can go wrong during a *simchah*, and were happy that things had gone right. But nothing could prepare them for what happened next.

Sarah changed into more comfortable clothing and sat down at the table to have a cup of tea with her husband. Suddenly, there was a knock at the door. Sarah looked at her husband, wondering if he was expecting anyone, but he was as surprised as she was. They both got up to answer the door. Standing there was Mrs. Yankelewitz. Though Sarah was taken aback, she invited her in and asked if everything was all right.

"I really just came to thank you for the cake," the old woman said. "You have no idea how meaningful it was. The only person who ever remembered my birthday besides my husband was my sister. As you know, my husband died a long time ago. My sister was the only one left, and she died a few months ago. I am completely alone now, and I was so sad that there was nobody left to tell me 'Happy Birthday.' I know this sounds silly coming from an 80-year-old woman. You probably think that I should just grow up already. But it was more than just the birthday wish. You took time out of your very busy schedule to think of me. Sarah, I will never forget your kindness."

Sarah and her husband were overwhelmed. They offered to walk her home, but Mrs. Yankelewitz wouldn't let them. Before she left, she turned toward them once more, and her eyes were filled with tears — and endless gratitude.

When Rav Eliyahu Eliezer Dessler returned to England after visiting Eretz Yisrael, he shared an anecdote. On the night that a certain philanthropist was marrying off his child and outfitting each of his family members in new clothes, he arranged for all the children of the Diskin Orphanage to be outfitted with new clothing, as well. Rav Dessler was so impressed by this act of kindness; he said it must have come from the *kedushah* (holiness) of Eretz Yisrael.

He complimented the generous man on his act of *chesed*, and then he made a suggestion: "Next time, make sure to spend more money on the clothing that you buy for the orphans than you do for your own family. Your family is wearing their clothes only in this world, but the merit of the clothing you have purchased for the orphans will be yours in the World to Come."

LIMUD
HATORAH

SPARKLE AND SHINE

ROM THE BEGINNING OF 1904 UNTIL THE END OF 1905, thousands of teenage Jewish boys were snatched from *batei midrash* across Russia, without even being given time to say goodbye to their parents. They were equipped with guns and ammunition and sent to the front lines of Manchuria, to defend Mother Russia in the Russo-Japanese War.

Due to the stubbornness of their ruler, Czar Nicholas II, the Russian army suffered one devastating defeat after another. Although it was fairly clear from the outset that Russia would not win the war, over the course of a year and a half, thousands of soldiers — Jews and non-Jews — lost their lives. These terrified young men fought valiantly but were no match for their Japanese counterparts.

Many of the conscripted Jewish soldiers had a source of comfort and solace: their Rebbe, Rav Yehudah Aryeh Leib Alter, better known as the Sfas Emes.

Orphaned at the age of 8, Yehudah Aryeh Leib was raised by his grandfather, the famed Chiddushei HaRim, Rav Yitzchak Meir. Yehudah Aryeh Leib was only 18 years old when his grandfather passed away. Many wanted him to assume the role of leadership, but he managed to push them off for a few years. Finally, at the age of 23, the Sfas Emes assumed the mantle. By the time of the

Russo-Japanese War, his fame had spread throughout the Torah world.

He received tens of letters a day from the young soldiers who turned to him for encouragement. Each letter he read broke his heart. One young man wrote about a bloodbath of a battle he had been involved in, which took several of his closest friends. Some boys wrote about how they had lost arms, legs, and even eyes. Others lamented about their lack of ability to live a Chassidic lifestyle while in the army. He read these letters with a heavy heart and cried bitterly, for there was no way he could help them, except by offering a few words of encouragement and, of course, by davening for them. There was one letter that moved the Rebbe like no other.

The letter began, like many others, with great praises for the Rebbe, but instead of immediately launching into a description of the horrific battles, the young letter-writer from Ostrovtza quoted the Rashba in *Kiddushin* and asked an intricate question on his line of reasoning. He suggested one response and then disproved it with another strong question.

The Rebbe's eyes darted across the page. As he continued to read, tears filled his eyes, but a smile began to form on his lips. He could not believe what he was reading. There was no mention of the war, and no mention of the danger. The writer didn't complain about the physical pain or the suffering or the loneliness. He just wanted to share one of his *chiddushim* (novel Torah thoughts). That is what gave him comfort. That is what gave him hope.

The Rebbe asked his attendant for a quill and some parchment and wrote to the soldier in return.

"I received your letter, and I want you to know how impressed I was." He then quoted the verse in *Parashas Nitzavim* (*Devarim* 30:19): "*Ha'idosi vachem hayom es hashamayim ve'es ha'aretz* — I call heaven and earth today to bear witness against you." Simply understood, this means that heaven and earth will bear witness and testify that the Jewish people were warned of the consequences of sin. But the Sfas Emes, in his inimitable style, found a beautiful homiletic insight. The word *ha'idosi* contains the word *edi*, which means a jewel, an ornament.

He addressed the young man, "When young men like you don't worry about their grave situation and the danger in which they find themselves, but have the wherewithal and inner strength to concern themselves only with the *Aibeshter*'s Torah, He considers them as the *edi*, the ornaments, of heaven and earth. You, and those like you, are like the jewels of This World."

The Sfas Emes ended the letter with a heartfelt blessing for safety and a speedy return home. The letter reached the young man from Ostrovtza, who cherished it for the rest of his life.

The collective pain of these young men took their toll on the Sfas Emes. A little less than one year after the war began, before he even reached the age of 60, he returned his exalted soul to its Maker.

Although the vast majority of our young men are never asked to join the armies of other nations, thousands risk their lives on the battlefield — for the Jewish people in Eretz Yisrael. It is truly inspiring to see how many of them are able to set aside time to daven with a minyan. In fact, a talmid of mine, who was fighting in Gaza during Operation Protective Edge, shared with me, "After we are finished fighting, I try to steal a few moments to give a Daf Yomi shiur."

At the same time, when the young men of today's generation are faced with unimaginable temptations and wage their spiritual battles against the diabolical schemes of the yetzer hara, they, too, fight with the bravery of soldiers on the front lines, unwilling as they are to conform to the norms of secular society.

The primary focus of their lives remains Torah study, as they sparkle and shine — like jewels — throughout heaven and earth.

NOT SO RANDOM CODES

ASIDE FROM HIS WORK FOR THE VAAD HATZALAH AND the efforts he invested in saving thousands of Jews during World War II, Rav Michoel Ber Weissmandl was a giant in Torah and a genius in original thought. Well before there were any Torah Codes, he devised his own — without the use of a computer — in ways that boggle the mind.

Once, before Purim, Rav Michoel Ber and his dear friend, Rav Mordechai Grunwald, spent some time together exchanging Torah thoughts on Purim. Rav Michoel Ber then asked Rav Mordechai what appeared to be a random question: "Have you counted how many letters there are in *Megillas Esther*?"

Rav Mordechai was not surprised by the question; he knew of Rav Michoel Ber's fascination with numbers as they apply to the Torah. When he responded that he did not know how many letters there were, Rav Michoel Ber smiled and said, "There are 12,196 letters in the *Megillah*."

Rav Mordechai sensed that Rav Michoel Ber had more to tell him, so he asked him, "What am I supposed to do with that number?"

Rav Michoel Ber then shared a fascinating code. If one were to begin from the first time the letter *aleph* appears in the Torah (in the word *Bereishis*) and count 12,196 letters, he would come to the letter *samach*. From there, if he were to count another 12,196 letters, he would arrive at the letter *tav*. And finally, another 12,196 letters would bring him to the letter *reish*. This, of course, spells out the word אסתר.

Rav Mordechai had come to expect such computations from his dear friend. He then asked him in jest, "What is Mordechai [of the *Megillah*] going to do? Isn't he going to be upset that Esther is mentioned in code and he is not?"

Rav Michoel Ber smiled at his friend's question, but recommended that they wait another year before he reveals his answer. The following year, Rav Michoel Ber shared another code, no less remarkable than the first one.

The Gemara finds an allusion to Mordechai HaTzaddik in the Torah. One of the spices in the *ketores* (incense) is *mor dror*, pure myrrh (*Shemos* 30:23). This is rendered by *Targum* as *meira dachya*, which sounds like *Mordechai*. If one were to begin from the letter *mem* in that *pasuk* and count 12,196 letters, he would reach the letter *reish*. If he were to count 12,196 letters three more times consecutively, he would reach the letters *dalet, chaf,* and then *yud*, spelling the word מרדכי.

This thought brought a wide smile to both of their faces.

But that is not the end of the story.

A number of years later, there was an outreach seminar for Jews of all backgrounds. One woman in particular expressed interest in improving her observance. However, since she was of an intellectual bent, she could not get over certain questions pertaining to the Torah itself. The leaders of the seminar decided that it would be best for her to experience a Shabbos in a warm and healthy environment. To that end, she spent a Shabbos at the home of Rav Mordechai Grunwald. Even at the Grunwalds' Shabbos table, no matter how hard the family members tried, they could not convince her of the truth of the Torah, that it was *min haShamayim* — from Heaven. In her mind, her questions remained unanswered.

Since it was Purim time, Rav Mordechai shared the thought he had heard years before from Rav Michoel Ber. She listened intently and was astounded. When she came out of her room the next morning, she seemed exhausted, as if she hadn't slept at all. When asked why she was so tired, she explained, "My expertise is mathematics. I stayed up the entire night, calculating the probability of such a random code. After a number of hours, I came to the conclusion that the chance of this happening randomly is zero."

Yet when she said goodbye, she still appeared uncommitted.

Years later, Rav Grunwald attended a wedding with his wife. Immediately after the *chuppah*, a woman named Esther approached them. She told them that she was the woman who had spent a Shabbos at their home. They would never have recognized her. Her hair was covered, and she was proud to tell them that she and her husband, Mordechai, were living a Torah life, and raising their children according to the Torah; she kept a kosher kitchen and her children were learning in a yeshivah.

*Yes, **Mordechai** and **Esther** Weissfeld were living a life of Torah Jews.*
And their children were learning Torah min HaShamayim.

THE SECRET ACCOUNT

WHEN RAV CHAIM KREISWIRTH WAS A YOUNG MAN, he was already renowned as a brilliant Torah scholar who impressed even the greatest *talmidei chachamim* of prewar Europe. Rav Meir Shapiro, Rav Chaim Ozer Grodzenski, and Rav Chanoch Eiges (the author of the *Marcheshes*) all spent time with him and came out of their meetings duly impressed. But Rav Chaim was more than just a scholarly Talmudic genius. His sterling character traits earned him a reputation as a *gaon* in *middos*, as well. Rav Avrohom Grodzenski, the mashgiach of the Slabodka Yeshivah, was so taken with Rav Chaim that he offered him his daughter's hand in marriage. A short while later, they were married.

But as war raged through Europe, the Nazis overtook city by city, and the Kreiswirths' blissful existence came to an abrupt end.

One day, the men of his town were called to the town square. Rav Chaim reported along with the others, though he was not chosen to be taken away for "work" — just yet. Rav Chaim watched with great sorrow as the men were led away. Those chosen knew the horrible fate that awaited them.

Suddenly, one of the wealthier people of the city called out to him. When Rav Chaim turned toward the fellow, he handed him a piece of paper. On it, the man explained, were the numbers of the Swiss bank accounts that he had established. He knew that he would most likely not survive, but he hoped that someone from his family would survive the war. Knowing that Rav Chaim was a responsible individual, the man asked him to deliver the information to his children, if and when he found them after the war. Rav Chaim assured the worried fellow that he would be a trustworthy messenger.

This was easier said than done.

Within weeks, the Nazis evacuated the town and murdered all of its inhabitants. Although Rav Chaim and his wife escaped, no one else from the city was so fortunate; they met their tragic end like millions of their brothers and sisters. Even though Rav Chaim lost nearly all of his worldly possessions while on the run, he vigilantly guarded the paper with which he had been entrusted. After the war, he tried to find out if any of the wealthy man's children had survived, but his quests repeatedly came up empty.

Rav Chaim eventually moved to Belgium and served as the *av beis din* in the city of Antwerp. Many years later, while he was learning in the *beis midrash*, an unkempt beggar walked in, sat down at the end of one of the benches, and asked people for money as they came and went. Rav Chaim handed him some money and asked him his name and where he came from.

When the man responded, Rav Chaim turned white as a sheet. He could not believe it. This beggar was the wealthy man's child. Just to be sure, he asked the fellow questions about his family, until it was clear that he was indeed the man's son.

Rav Chaim sat down next to the fellow and told him the entire story: about how his father had given him the numbers to his secret accounts in Switzerland, and how he had held onto them for 20 years, searching for a surviving relative. Then he handed him all the information that he needed.

The fellow could not believe his eyes. He stared at the numbers and thanked Rav Chaim profusely for all he had done for his father, and now for him. He took the first train to Switzerland he could find, and retrieved all of the money his father had put aside for him.

After Rav Chaim told the story, he added: For 20 years, while this beggar wandered in torn and ripped clothing, begging for food and sleeping on park benches, he was actually a very wealthy individual; he had millions of dollars waiting for him in Swiss bank accounts. There was only one problem: he had no idea that the treasure existed. He never knew he was anything but a beggar. If only he had known about the treasure earlier, those 20 years of his life could have been spent in comfort and enjoyment, instead of in suffering and misery.

The very same is true for all of us. All we need is the secret code to claim our treasures. The secret code is called the Torah, and by unlocking its secrets, we can live our lives in the Next World in unimaginable spiritual luxury.

What a waste it would be if we never took the opportunity to realize how very rich we are.

A LATE-NIGHT PHONE CALL

W HEN RABBI SHALOM FRIEDMAN ASKED ME TO travel to a large city in the Midwest for the final night of Chanukah, I was a bit hesitant. I did not want to leave my family, and I tried to push him off for a different time. However, in his own convincing way, he conveyed the importance of coming for this particular event: a *siyum* for his morning *kollel*. He told me that many of the *mesayemim* (those making the *siyum*) would be finishing a *masechta* (tractate) for the first time in their lives. Sensing that it would be a memorable evening, I agreed to go. I would not be disappointed.

At the time, the *kollel boker* (morning *kollel*) was comprised of young married men, who, for the most part, had not spent the first few years of their marriage in full-time learning. But a year before this *siyum*, everything changed for them. It was obvious that many of them were very proud of their accomplishments. The singing and the speeches conveyed this sentiment, as well. The participants were inspired and were now eager to begin the next *masechta*.

After my speech, two people came to share their stories. The first fellow told me that it was a very important night for him; it was the first time he had ever really finished anything. Yes, when he was 13 years old, his father had someone else read a *masechta* while he sat across from him — so that he could officially make a *siyum*. But as he put it, that would hardly count as having learned a *masechta*. Although he had attended yeshivos, he had never been successful. I listened in amazement, wondering how difficult it must have been for a fellow in his early 30's to begin learning Torah seriously. I told him how incredibly proud I was of him. In truth, I was jealous of him for being able to summon the necessary discipline, after all these years, to finish a *masechta*.

A second fellow told me a story that may have had an even greater impact on me. When he was in 11th grade, this boy was told by his rebbi that he was no longer cut out for their yeshivah. But unfortunately, the rebbi didn't stop there. He told the vulnerable young man that he wasn't really cut out for learning in *any* yeshivah, and that he should set his sights on something else. Perhaps the saddest part of the story is that the rebbi did not realize how hurtful his words were. Finishing this *masechta* proved to this man that he *was* able to learn, and that he was cut out for learning. It was a redemption of sorts. I was very moved by his story.

By this point, I was happy that I had come. But nothing could have prepared me for what I would hear next.

I went over to the main organizer of the event, the one who had sponsored most of it, and thanked him for inviting me. When I asked him how the *kollel* had started, I was pointed in the direction of the coordinator's *chavrusa*. I was well acquainted with this *chavrusa* from my years in camp, so I felt comfortable asking him to tell me his part. This is the story he was happy to share with me:

> I was at a very bad point in my life, and I was struggling spiritually. One night, at the holiday company party, my boss asked to speak to me. He explained that when he hires someone, he takes upon himself the responsibility of supporting and caring for the welfare of that employee and his family, in a material sense as well as in a spiritual sense. He had noticed that I was struggling with my spirituality, and he hoped to see a vast improvement. He had a practical way to go about this, too: "Show up a half-hour before davening tomorrow, for a half-hour seder with a chavrusa. Davening starts at 7:30, so be there at 7."
>
> I wasn't interested in the whole conversation to begin

with. I told him in no uncertain terms that my spirituality was none of his business. But he wasn't fazed, and he told me he would see me at 7 a.m.

I left the party in a really bad mood. I was very upset that my boss was getting involved where he did not belong. And then, at 1:30 in the morning, the phone rang. Who would be calling me at this hour? I looked at my phone, and I saw that it was my boss on the line. When I picked up, he said to me, "I didn't get the name of your chavrusa." I couldn't believe it. I gave some snide retort and hung up the phone.

Two hours later, at 3:30 in the morning, the phone rang once more. It was my boss again. I was very, very angry. When I answered, I screamed, "How in the world am I supposed to find a chavrusa at 3:30 a.m.?"

He very calmly replied, "Sometimes the answers to life's biggest problems are right in front of you. I will be your chavrusa. Make sure that you are there on time. We're starting at 7."

"That was almost a year ago," he concluded. "Since then, we have finished five *masechtos,* and we haven't missed one day. At times, we were on two different continents, but 7 o'clock is 7 o'clock. The *kollel* started with just the two of us. Soon after we began, a few more fellows joined, and now we are up to 35 participants. Not only that, but after davening, we have a small *chaburah* [group discussion] where we learn halachah."

I listened in awe. To think that the perseverance of one individual and the commitment of his downtrodden employee could blossom into such a great *kiddush Hashem* (sanctification of Hashem's Name). I thanked him for the story and thanked him for opening up to me.

A few months later, I was privileged to speak at a *melaveh malkah* at Kahal Tiferes Yaakov, which is led by Rav Avrohom Schorr. I discussed the concept of being part of a *tzibbur* (congregation), and how we must all feel a responsibility for one another; in line with this theme, I told the above story.

As soon as I finished, Rav Schorr got up to speak. He said that he was "touched" by many of the stories, but that this particular story struck a chord with him. He was so inspired that he announced right there and then that he would be starting his own *kollel boker* the following morning.

> *As this story is being written, there are nearly 50 young men in the first city who have joined this remarkable initiative. To their credit and to the credit of their wives, they come every morning to learn. And they will be the first to tell you that it has changed their lives. I recently spoke to Rav Schorr, and he told me that his kollel boker is still going strong, as well.*
>
> *I don't usually make predictions, but I feel it is safe to say that people will read this story and will be inspired to do something about it. I imagine that the first kollel boker, and the one in Flatbush, will influence others to set up morning kollelim in their shuls. And there is no telling how many lives can be changed.*
>
> *All because of one boss who refused to give up, and an employee who agreed to listen.*

GUARDING THE NIGHT

AT THE TURN OF THE 20TH CENTURY, THERE WAS A courtyard near Shaar Shechem called Chatzar Strauss. In this modest enclave lived some of the greatest *tzaddikim*. They lived a life of modesty, with one purpose in mind: to serve Hashem in the best way that they could.

Among this group was a *tzaddik* by the name of Rav Tzvi Hirsch Weissfish; he was a *talmid* of Rav Tzvi Michel Shapiro and a grandson of Rav Nachum Shadiker. Rav Tzvi Hirsch spent a tremendous amount of time in prayer, and he fasted often. Very few people were aware of this in his lifetime, as he shunned all attention and tried his utmost to stay out of the limelight.

One night, at approximately midnight and after a long evening of learning, a young Simchah Zissel Brodie, who later became the rosh yeshivah of the Chevron Yeshivah, was walking with his father toward their apartment in Chatzar Strauss.

In the distance, he saw Rav Tzvi Hirsch Weissfish. Rav Weissfish was standing in front of some posters. These were posters that publicized the various events — such as concerts and shows — that were going on around town. As strange as it seemed, the *tzaddik* was not only wasting his time reading them, but he seemed genuinely interested in the specific details of when these events were taking place.

As Simchah Zissel came closer, he became more certain that his eyes were not fooling him. He noticed that Rav Tzvi Hirsch's gaze was fixated on one particular event. The following night, there was going to be a festival in a small village right near Yam HaMelach. The Dead Sea was a popular area, with many restaurants, cafés, and coffeehouses in the vicinity. The poster promised dancing and music "from sunset to sunrise." Simchah Zissel was completely dumbfounded by what he saw. Was it possible that Rav Tzvi Hirsch would have the slightest interest in this indecent and impure dancing festival?

That night, the disturbing image kept recurring in Simchah Zissel's mind. He knew better than to question the piety of this *tzaddik,* but the utter confusion caused him a sleepless night.

The next morning, Simchah Zissel went to daven at the *vasikin* (sunrise) *minyan*; there were no other *minyanim* in that neighborhood. His father, who had watched Rav Tzvi Hirsch along with him, knew that he was very bothered. He decided that he was going to ask Rav Tzvi Hirsch about the incident directly. Together with his son, he walked over to Rav Tzvi Hirsch. However, before they had a chance to express their curiosity, the *tzaddik* realized what was troubling them. Although he normally would not have divulged his activities, he felt it was important for them to know what was going on.

"I am part of a group of seven men. We have taken upon ourselves to do battle with the *yetzer hara*. Whenever we see him fully at work, each of us, on a rotating basis, takes a day to fight him. We scout the streets to find out what inappropriate events are taking place in Eretz Yisrael. Then we try to offset that impurity with an extra dose of holiness and sanctity. This is the only way we can protect our holy land, by guarding it from the infidels who want to destroy it.

"During our watch, it is forbidden to eat, drink, sleep, or do anything except learn Torah. We cannot, and we must not, allow the *yetzer hara* to dance together with our children.

"Yesterday, I saw the poster publicizing an event near *Yam HaMelach*. I was checking the exact times because tonight is my turn. I must know the exact time that the festival will take place, so I can combat those forces of evil with acts of *kedushah*."

> Many years later, Rav Simchah Zissel, a giant in his own right, told over the story and emphasized the importance of every person doing his part. We must not get discouraged from the power of our opponent. It is daunting for one person to try to do everything himself. However, if each person does his small part, then eventually we will be able to slay the giant that is the yetzer hara.

PRICELESS POTATOES

RAV CHIZKIYAHU MISHKOVSKY, THE MASHGIACH OF Yeshiva Orchos Torah and Gaon Yaakov, was acquainted with a man named Rav Goldstein. Rav Goldstein had an unusual love for Torah and immense respect for those who learned it. Rav Mishkovsky was intrigued by Rav Goldstein's extraordinary *ahavas haTorah* (love for Torah), and asked him if a specific occurrence had brought it about.

Rav Goldstein closed his eyes, as if he were transporting himself back to a different time and a different era, and told the following story:

> *Our family lived in Hungary, which, at first, remained relatively unscathed even as Hitler conquered most of Europe. In 1944, though, everything changed — and quickly. My father was one of the first to be taken for work detail. Or that is what they told us. But we soon found out that my father was killed immediately, together with many others. Before long, the Nazis began to systematically exterminate all of Hungarian Jewry.*
>
> *Finally, only my mother, my brother, and I were left. My mother did her very best to protect us, but eventually we were placed on a train headed for Auschwitz. From there, we were to be taken directly to the gas chambers. We were just young children and we did not know this at the time, but my mother most certainly did.*
>
> *For some reason, however, the harrowing train ride did not bring us to our intended destination. Instead, we were redirected to a location approximately 20 kilometers from Auschwitz.*
>
> *The soldiers were angry at this turn of events, which*

forced all of us to walk the rest of the way. Food was scarce and we had eaten very little over the last few days. As we began the trek, my mother saw that my brother and I were too weak to make it. Determined to save our lives, she held us both in her arms. It must have been incredibly difficult for her; we were not little babies, and she had also hardly eaten in days.

As we walked on the road, the Nazi guards yelled at us constantly, letting out their frustration upon us, while the dogs' incessant barking terrified us. At one point, we passed a non-Jewish woman. Horrified by what she saw, she was overcome with compassion and ran over to my mother to give her a bag of potatoes. However, as she handed it to my mother, a Nazi guard warned her that if she gave the sack to my mother, he would shoot her.

The woman had no choice but to hold it in her arms. Nevertheless, in a show of solidarity, she continued to walk with us. Then, when the guard was not looking, she slipped two potatoes into my mother's hand. My mother thanked her for the precious gift, and the woman slipped away before the guard noticed what had happened.

Instead of giving one potato to my brother and one to me, my mother handed one to me and instructed me to give the potato to an elderly gentleman with a long beard. She told me his name was Rav Moshe Stern, and that he was the dayan (judge) in Debrecen and a very big talmid chacham. She said that he would insist that I keep the potato, and that I should tell him that my mother says she has an extra one.

I did as I was told, using whatever strength I had to walk over to the rav. Sure enough, he didn't want to accept the potato, but when I told him that it was an extra one, he thanked me profusely and accepted it. I went back to my mother and we walked together, with newfound strength, content to share one potato between the three of us. Then my mother stated decisively, "That is what we do for a talmid chacham."

"Miraculously," concluded Rav Goldstein, "we survived the war and made our way to Eretz Yisrael. Although this story happened so many years ago, I will never forget the *mesirus nefesh* (personal sacrifice) my mother displayed for a *talmid chacham*. She taught me that Torah is the most important thing in the world."

Rav Goldstein had tears streaming down his face as he recalled the story from so long ago. But he smiled at Rav Chizkiyahu and stated emphatically, "That is how I acquired my *ahavas haTorah*."

AN IMPENETRABLE WALL

The following story took place 400 years ago, in the city of Istanbul, Turkey. Its lesson is as applicable today as when it happened.

THEY WERE THE BEST OF FRIENDS. AHARON ELKARIF and Menachem Benbisti were inseparable. They played in each other's homes, sharing common interests. They sat next to each other in school. Wherever you saw one, you saw the other. All the boys in their city looked up to the two friends and admired their closeness.

The two of them grew older, and the time came for them to get married. Menachem married a girl from the Senyora family. The Senyoras had a successful business, and they promised to support him for a long time. Menachem only wanted to learn, and their daughter, Rosa, shared his vision.

The first few months of their marriage were like a dream. While Menachem utilized every spare moment for his learning, his wife helped out in the business; she felt that it was her responsibility to pitch in. She was very grateful that her parents agreed to support her and her husband, and she wanted to do her part, too.

But then, everything changed. The family business began to decline. Rosa's father did whatever he could to control the losses, but each venture he entered failed miserably. At the same time, other businesses sprouted and became successful. Although the Senyoras had promised to take care of their son-in-law and daughter, it seemed that they were no longer able to.

Menachem's wife assured him that her parents were not going to stop their support just because the business was not doing well. Yet Menachem saw how his in-laws were struggling, and he began to rethink his commitments. Perhaps he should help out for a few hours each day in the business; he was sharp and possessed real business acumen.

At first, he hoped to work for a few months, until the business got back on its feet. Indeed, within a few weeks, his fresh ideas helped revitalize the struggling enterprise. However, after a few months, the notion of him returning to full-time learning became a distant reality. He was extremely successful, and he became sucked into the world of business.

In the meantime, his best friend, Aharon, also got married, to a girl from the Fredo family. Reb Natan, his father-in-law, owned a beautiful shul, which boasted the prominent citizens of the city as its members. Aharon was offered the opportunity to open a yeshivah inside the shul, where he could spend his entire day learning and teaching. He eagerly accepted the position. Each week, he delivered many lectures to the young men of Istanbul.

One would have expected that now that Menachem and Aharon had gone their separate ways, they would no longer have anything to do with each other. But nothing could be further from the truth.

Although it was a challenge for Menachem to find time to learn, he still felt the pull of the *beit midrash*. Thus, once the business had regained its footing, he asked his best friend if they could learn together every day. How could Aharon turn down his best friend?

And so, they made up to learn for four hours every day. That's right, four hours! Menachem was overjoyed with the arrangement.

No matter what was going on in their lives, the two of them learned every night from 6 to 10. During those four hours, in which they plumbed the depths of the Gemara, the world did not exist. Nothing and no one could disturb them and take away that precious time.

It was as if there was a wall surrounding the two of them, which no one could penetrate.

As strong as the relationship was before, it was 10 times stronger now. The bond of their learning strengthened their friendship. This continued for decades. Those who had marveled over their friendship when they were young derived tremendous satisfaction observing the two of them as they learned together, and as they blossomed into leaders of the community.

Both Reb Menachem and Reb Aharon were blessed with children and grandchildren. Of course, they experienced ups and downs in their lives. But through it all, there was one constant: their learning.

As they neared the age of 80, they thought about how difficult it would be for them to part from each other. They had overcome so much together. Who could imagine Hashem taking one soul without taking the other?

The two of them made a pact. Whoever died first would come back to the other one and tell him what he found on the Other Side. They made a special *tekias kaf* (handshake) to seal the agreement.

One night, on the cusp of completing his ninth decade, Reb Menachem Elkarif learned with Reb Aharon as usual. Then he went home and went to sleep. The next morning, he was no longer alive.

Reb Aharon cried uncontrollably at the funeral. A part of his life was now gone. Yet he knew that because of their agreement, he would be seeing his friend soon.

One night, before 30 days had passed, Reb Aharon was sitting at his Gemara learning. Alone. Then he dozed off. Suddenly, he saw his best friend, Reb Menachem. He was smiling, just as he had his entire life.

"Menachem," Reb Aharon said to his friend, "tell me how it went. What happened when you came to heaven? What is it like in the World to Come?"

Reb Menachem replied, "To tell you the truth, a soul is usually not granted permission to descend from heaven. From the moment that my soul left your world, its connection was severed. However, because we made a *tekias kaf,* I was obligated to come back down. I am sorry, but I am unable to tell you all that takes place in the Next World. I am only allowed to tell you what happened to me personally."

After I died, all of my family members who had died before me came to greet me. Then there was an announcement: "Anyone who has anything to say about Menachem should come forward and testify." Thousands of angels, both good and bad, came forward and described what I had done in my life. The good malachim spoke glowingly about all the wonderful things I had accomplished. But then, the malachei chavalah [angels of destruction] stepped forward and screamed at me, embarrassing me for the sins I had committed throughout my lifetime. I was so ashamed in front of my family, who witnessed the entire scene. I wanted to hide, but there was nowhere to go. The destructive angels counted each and every one of my sins, and I trembled.

Suddenly, a wall came down out of nowhere and separated me from those terrible angels. A thundering voice echoed through the court and proclaimed that I was found innocent.

I couldn't believe it. After the long and detailed list of sins I had committed, how was I proclaimed innocent? Where had that wall come from? I was told that it was created by our fierce commitment and unfailing dedication to Torah study. Every day that we learned, another brick was added to the wall.

It was specifically our kevius (consistency) that fortified and strengthened the wall, and made it impenetrable. Even when it was snowing, raining, or excessively hot; even when we were incredibly tired; through sickness and sorrow; through worry and anxiety…we never gave up on those four hours.

Had we allowed those occurrences to penetrate our commitment, the angels may have been able to break through, as well. However, since nothing ever stopped us from our learning, nothing they said could harm me.

My dearest Aharon, this is the only thing that I am permitted to tell you from the Other Side. Appreciate the power of our kevius for learning, and tell others, as well. Pass it on to future generations. For this information is a priceless gift.

With that, Menachem left his lifelong friend for the last time.

Of course, it is challenging to keep to a schedule of learning. But if we want to be protected, we must continue to build our wall — no matter what.

THE BREAD BASKET

Rav Aryeh Pleshnitzki, a maggid shiur in Yeshivas Shaarei Yosher and author of the sefer Askinu Seudasa, told the following story:

BEFORE WORLD WAR II, YESHIVAS OHEL TORAH OF BARAnovich, which was led by Rav Elchanan Wasserman, was known as one of the premier places of learning for teenage boys. For these *talmidim,* Baranovich was an important step on their way to greatness.

Rav Tzvi Hirsch Gutman, the *menahel* (principal), was a tremendous *talmid chacham.* He had received a ringing endorsement from the Steipler Gaon, who testified that he was an expert in all four sections of *Shulchan Aruch.*

Rav Gutman viewed his responsibility to each and every boy as a personal one. At that time, the *menahel* would often shoulder the obligation for both the spiritual and physical welfare of the *talmidim.* Hence, it was Rav Tzvi Hirsch who made sure each boy had a place to eat as well as a place to sleep.

During the period between World War I and World War II, Europe was mired in a deep financial crisis. As *menahel,* Rav Gutman left no stone unturned as he tried to raise the necessary funds. Despite all those efforts, there were times when the young men did not eat a normal supper. They would go to bed hungry, but wake the next morning with a fresh desire to resume their studies, displaying true sacrifice for their learning.

Rav Tzvi Hirsch was very troubled about the difficulties the *talmidim* had to endure. Left with no other choice, he decided to travel overseas in order to raise money. The thought of starving young men sacrificing themselves for their learning pushed him not to give up.

From a young age, the Gutman children understood the importance of learning, and they wanted to help their father. Two of his daughters, Chana Rochel and Sarah Baila, who were 20 and 16 years old respectively, took matters into their own hands. One day, when their father was out of the country, the two of them went out to the streets of the city with large baskets in their hands. They went from door to door, asking the townspeople if they could spare some bread for the yeshivah boys. Their heartfelt pleas made an impression, and soon their baskets began to fill up — with bread and other types of food. Although it was embarrassing for the girls to go around begging, they were willing to overcome their shame for the sake of the *talmidim's* Torah study.

As they went from house to house, Rav Elchanan happened to pass them, and their actions caught his attention. He walked over to the young ladies and asked them what they were doing. They informed him that this was their way of helping the yeshivah.

Rav Elchanan was touched by their actions, and moved by their sacrifice for *limud Torah*. He was impressed that they were able to overcome their shame for the sake of the young men. He blessed them that they should merit long lives, and that they should see their children, grandchildren, and future generations growing higher and higher in their *limud* and *ahavas haTorah*.

Not long thereafter, the clouds of war darkened the skies of Europe, and the continent became drenched in Jewish blood. Six million Jews perished, among them the great Rav Elchanan, who was shot together with his *talmidim*, and Rav Tzvi Hirsch, who was killed along with most of his family.

Based on the advice of Rav Elchanan, Chana Rochel had emigrated to Eretz Yisrael before the war. She married Rav Shmuel Felman, a close *talmid* of the Chazon ish. After the war, she wanted nothing more than to rebuild her family.

Chana Rochel thought that she was the only family member who had survived. Only after a number of years did she find out that her sister, Sarah Baila, had also escaped the clutches of the Nazis. She married Rav Mendel Kaplan, a beloved rebbi in Talmudical Yeshiva of Philadelphia.

The blessing of Rav Elchanan was fulfilled. Both sisters merited offspring who enjoyed a great love for Torah, and they both lived very long lives. On the fifth day of Adar, 5764, Chana Rochel passed away at the ripe old age of 98. Four years later, on the very same day, her younger sister passed away. She, too, was 98 years old.

After her death, one of the *gedolim* who came to comfort Rebbetzin Felman's children pointed out that at the age of 20, Chana

Rochel had collected bread, *lechem,* whose numerical value is 78. Hence, Hashem rewarded her with 78 additional years.

Four years later, it became obvious that her younger sister received 82 additional years of life, the numerical value of the word *banayich* — your sons.

No action or sacrifice goes unrewarded.

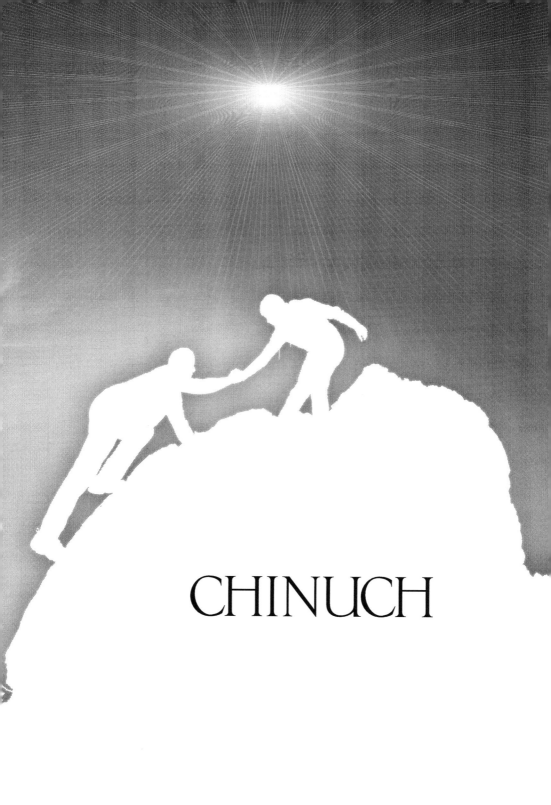

CHINUCH

CAUSE FOR CELEBRATION

LTHOUGH RAV DOVID BRAVERMAN HAD MANY THINGS to do on Erev Rosh Hashanah, he agreed to speak in the local yeshivah for teenage American boys. However, when he walked into the building, he was surprised that no one was in the *beis midrash*. What was even more surprising was the loud music coming from down the hall. He followed his ears until he found himself in the dining room, which was bustling with activity.

He saw the boys dancing with great vigor and excitement. It wasn't only the boys who were dancing: the rebbeim and roshei yeshivah encircled them and danced along with them. After looking around the room for a few moments, Rav Dovid spied the rosh yeshivah, approached him, and asked him what was going on. The rosh yeshivah realized that the entire scene looked somewhat strange: a full-blown party on Erev Rosh Hashanah! So he stepped outside with Rav Dovid for a moment and explained:

> *We have a bachur in our yeshivah who is really a very good boy. He learns well and does everything he is supposed to. He is full of yiras Shamayim, and for the most part, he has very good character traits. But there used to be one very big problem. He was a kaasan: he had a temper. It's not that he walked*

around all day in a bad mood. But when he got upset, he could not control his temper and lashed out at people. This was a problem because a lot of the boys didn't want to have anything to do with him. But there was an even bigger problem: he felt like a total failure. The fact that he was unable to control himself caused him to feel down and depressed.

We spoke to him on a number of occasions, but he just could not get hold of himself. Finally, I decided to do something drastic.

I called him into my office and handed him an envelope containing $500 cash, and I told him, "You are a wonderful boy. You have so many things going for you, but you know that you have this one big issue that we need to get under control. I really believe that you can do it. Inside this envelope is $500. This is not the yeshivah's money; it comes from my personal funds.

"This is what we are going to do. You are going to work on yourself to make sure that you don't lose your temper over the next year. I am not going to speak to you about it at all. But if you work on this for a full year, then next year, one year from tonight, I will give you the money to keep."

The bachur didn't want to take the envelope, but I told him that I am so confident that he is going to succeed that I want him to have the money now. He took the money, albeit reluctantly, and that was the last time we spoke about this issue for a full year.

Last night he came over to me and asked to speak to me privately. Then he put the envelope on the table and began to cry. I picked up the envelope and read the note that was written on it.

It said:

"Dear Rebbi, I am very grateful that you gave me a chance to work on controlling my temper. Unfortunately, though I tried time and time again to control myself, I failed miserably.

I wish things would have worked out differently. Thank you so much for giving me the chance. I am so sorry that I disappointed you. With much appreciation, Your talmid."

I read the letter and tears filled my eyes, as well. I looked at him and saw that he was very broken. But I knew that he was wrong. I knew that he had tried really hard. So I asked him, "Tell me: How many times did you lose your temper over the course of the year?"

He mumbled that he did not know. But I pressed on. "I don't believe you. I don't believe that you don't know how many times you lost your temper, because I know how hard you must have worked at it. I am certain that every day was a struggle and you worked hard to control yourself. So please tell me. How many times did you lose your temper over the course of the year?"

He was quiet for a long while, and then finally he said in a very sad voice, "I lost my temper 48 times; I am so upset with myself. I failed repeatedly, throughout the year."

I could only imagine how painful this was for him, but I responded, "So let me make a quick calculation. If you failed 48 times, then the other 317 days of the year, you succeeded. Is that correct?"

He looked at me in disbelief. "But I lost my cool 48 times during the year. That is failure."

But I argued with him. "No! Why look at the amount of times you failed, when you can look at the amount of times you succeeded? And you succeeded 317 times: a rousing success by my estimation."

He was quiet. I sensed that he was starting to believe what I was telling him, so I continued. "This is what I am going to do. I am so proud of your incredible efforts and so satisfied with the results that I am not just going to give you the $500. Rather, I am going to make a huge celebration for you tomorrow night. We are going to celebrate the fact that you *were able to be maavir al midosav, to overcome your negative traits."*

The rosh yeshivah said to Reb Dovid, "That is why we are dancing tonight. With the *bachur's* permission, we are celebrating his efforts, for he invested immeasurable effort to conquer the demons of anger that haunted him. And when a young man works on himself that much, that is cause for celebration. He wants his friends to participate because they helped him get to where he is today, and everyone can learn from someone who conquers his *yetzer hara*."

We all have our shortcomings. And when we work on ourselves, it is crucial to appreciate even the small movements we make toward perfecting our characters.

The mere fact that we are working on ourselves can be reason enough to celebrate.

RIGHT MESSAGE, WRONG ADDRESS

IT WAS A VERY SPECIAL EVENING INDEED. THE ORGANIZAtion known as Le'Chaim! has helped many families of children who are diagnosed with terminal illnesses. Now, those people who benefitted from this special organization gathered to pay tribute to the man who established the organization, Chaim Bordonsky. Chaim was only 9 when he was diagnosed with cancer, and now, 25 years later, he was very happy that he had merited helping other families through the same difficult circumstances that he and his family had endured.

Though he was the guest of honor at the organization's first dinner, he did not want to take any of the credit himself. As he got up to accept his award, he thanked Hashem for bringing him to this very day. He expressed his appreciation to his parents, relatives, friends, and all the people who had supported him throughout his two years of treatment. He thanked his teachers and school administrators. He even conveyed his gratitude to the other patients who were in the hospital with him; they had become his lifelong friends, and they, too, had come out that evening to show their love and support.

Above all, he wanted to thank his doctors and nurses, who held his hand and helped him every step of the way. Before he even began his regimen, they patiently explained to him and his family the intricacies and challenges of the treatments he was about to endure, and they continued to be there for them as he lived through those difficult days. But at the end of the entire list of thank-you's, he thanked one doctor in particular, the doctor who originally diagnosed his illness: Dr. Elishar Cohen.

Then he proceeded to tell his audience just how Dr. Cohen had inspired him to find the wherewithal and the inner strength to fight, and how he instilled within him the hope that he would once again be healthy.

I had not been feeling well for many weeks, and had gone with my parents from one doctor to the next. Finally, after extensive blood tests, I was diagnosed with cancer. I still remember the look on my parents' faces when the doctors delivered the grim news. My parents could not believe it, and neither could I. I had heard the word before, but I never imagined that I would be stricken with that dreaded illness. Dr. Cohen spoke to us with such kindness and sensitivity, as he detailed the plan and told us what we needed to know.

Then he spoke to me privately. He explained that many
people lose their hair from the chemotherapy treatments, but
there was nothing to be afraid of. He answered all of my ques-
tions and assured me that everything would be all right.

After a long meeting, Dr. Cohen walked all of us to the
door of his office. As he opened the door, he said to the nurse
who was standing right there, "Tir'i, achoti, eizeh yeled im
koach — Take a look, nurse, at what strength this child has."

When I heard those words, I felt a boost of encouragement.
After hearing the details of the long, arduous road to recovery,
I was pleasantly surprised and very hopeful when he described
me as a strong boy. And that is what gave me the strength to
endure all the painful treatments over the next two years.

Chaim finished telling his story, and then called up Dr. Cohen
— to a standing ovation. He handed him a plaque and gave Dr.
Cohen a hug. The doctor, now in his 70's, stood at the podium and
waited for everyone to be seated.

"I know this is going to sound like a cliché, but I really don't
deserve this award. And I mean that in every sense of the word.
I know that you just heard a beautiful story about how I gave a
young boy hope by telling the nurse how strong he was. Indeed, I
remember that incident very well. I recall the meeting I had with
Chaim and his parents, and I remember telling him how he may
lose his hair during treatment. At the time, I experienced the sink-
ing feeling I got whenever I had to speak to a child about the horrific treatments he was about to face.

"In truth, I did not think that Chaim was going to make it. That's
right. I did not think that he was going to survive. I know that you
just heard the story about how I told the nurse that he was strong,
and that is true. But I have a confession to make. As he opened the
door, there was another child entering the office as Chaim was
leaving. And the comment I made was not intended for Chaim,
but for the boy who was entering the office at that very moment."

The crowd sat in stunned silence. Chaim turned to Dr. Cohen and smiled. The *Hashgachah* (Divine Providence) of it all was evident. Chaim had heard what Hashem wanted him to hear. And that gave him the strength to fight harder.

Chaim stood up and hugged Dr. Cohen, and thanked him for delivering the message that really was meant for him.

> *If we would give our children the impression that we honestly feel that each one is a "yeled im koach," imagine what they could accomplish. When they are infused with the knowledge that their parents really believe in them, they will strive even harder to reach their goals, and become the people they are meant to be.*

MOST IMPORTANT OF ALL

ONE DAY, RAV AVROHOM GANOCHOFSKY, THE ROSH yeshivah of the Tchebiner Yeshivah, walked in unannounced to the Lev L'Achim office in Yerushalayim. Shocked by the sudden appearance of the elderly rosh yeshivah, the staff members immediately asked what they could do for him. He stated simply that he had come to offer his services, and he was prepared to travel anywhere in the country if he could be of any help.

The people working in the office were humbled by his offer and apologetically informed him that at the moment, they did not need any help. Still eager to be of assistance, he informed them that if there was ever anything they needed, they should be in touch with him right away.

One evening, word reached the Lev L'Achim office that a Chinuch Atzmai school in the northern part of the country was in danger of closing due to lack of enrollment. The heads of Lev L'Achim remembered Rav Avrohom's generous offer, and they decided to recruit him. When he heard about the dire situation, Rav Avrohom agreed to help out; he would try to convince the school's headmaster that the school should remain open.

As soon as he hung up the phone, Rav Avrohom called the home of the headmaster and was informed that he was not available. Due to the tremendous strain he was under, he had decided to go to Teveriah for a few days in order to clear his mind. Rav Avrohom then informed the Lev L'Achim office that he was going to Teveriah to speak to the man. Not surprisingly, Rav Avrohom was prepared to go by bus, but they immediately sent a car for him.

When Rav Avrohom arrived in Teveriah and walked into the hotel, the headmaster was shocked to see him. He was moved that Rav Avrohom had taken it upon himself to personally visit him and beg him to keep the school open. But Rav Avrohom was not just speaking theoretically. He stated, "If the problem is money, then I am asking you to send me to any donor you want. Just give me the name, and I will travel there and ask him for the amount of money you need. I will even travel to *chutz la'Aretz* [out of the country]. But whatever you do, please don't let the school close."

The headmaster was overwhelmed by this selfless act of commitment and dedication. He assured Rav Avrohom that he would keep the school open no matter what.

A number of years later, Rav Avrohom spoke at a gathering in memory of Rav Chaim Brim, whom he admired and respected. Rav Avrohom and Rav Chaim were very similar. In fact, if one didn't know better, he could have thought that with the following anecdote, Rav Avrohom was eulogizing himself.

I had the privilege of knowing the niftar from the time that we were both young men in the Slabodka Yeshivah. Rav Chaim was a giant in Torah. He understood difficult and deep concepts with exceptional clarity. He was able to clarify complicated ideas in a sugya, and he was also able to see the depths of every Jewish soul. He sensed what they needed, and he helped them accomplish and achieve to their full potential.

One very cold and stormy winter night, when the hour was already very late, one of the principals of the local girls' school paid a visit to Rav Chaim's home. He told him about a young lady in his school who did not feel successful in her studies. She had left school and returned to her family's moshav a few days before. The principal was worried that because of her low self-esteem, she was never going to return to school. He was concerned for her future, that she may not remain a true bas Yisrael.

Rav Chaim listened very carefully, and a look of worry appeared on his face. He asked the principal for the name of the girl and her address. The principal explained that he did not have the address on him, but he would retrieve it from the school's office in the morning. Rav Chaim said that the matter could not wait even one extra minute. He decided to travel to the moshav and find her home once he got there. Though the hour was late and the weather was treacherous, Rav Chaim wrote down the girl's name, hopped into a taxi, and traveled toward her settlement. When he arrived, he still had no idea where to go. Then he saw a light on in one of the houses. Although the hour was really late by that time, he knocked on the door.

The residents opened the door and were startled to see such a prestigious person standing there. Rav Chaim apologized for the late hour and asked them if they knew where the young lady's family lived. They pointed him in the right direction and he headed straight for the home. When he arrived, the family members welcomed him into their home, though they *wondered what he could possibly being doing there at such a late hour.*

Rav Chaim asked to speak to the young lady. As she sat down across from him, she could not believe what she saw. He was drenched and clearly freezing from the cold temperature. Rav Chaim explained to her that he wanted her to go back to school, and that it would mean a lot to him if she did. When her mother assured him that she would be going back, he was not satisfied. He wanted to hear it from the girl herself. He told them that he would stay in the house until she agreed to go back. Realizing the tremendous sacrifice he had made to come out personally to ask her to come back to school, the young lady gave her word that she would go back to school the next day.

When he returned home later that night, Rav Chaim made a point of speaking to the school's administration, to make sure that they would shower her with extra love and care, so she would feel good about herself and feel successful.

She came back to school and turned over a new leaf.

Now, many years later, she is the mother of a large and beautiful family of bnei Torah.

Rav Chaim had numerous reasons not to go. He did not know where she lived and the weather was terrible. He could have said that she would not listen to him. But all of those reasons paled in comparison to the one reason that he should go: he had a chance to save her life.

And nothing in the world was more important than that.

The Lesson From the Ledger

Rav Moshe Aryeh Freund traveled with a group of men to Eastern Europe, to visit the graves of some of his ancestors and other tzaddikim. In their travels, the group came to the city of Lemberg, where many great Jews are buried in the ancient cemetery, among them Rav David HaLevi Segal, known as the Taz, who served as the rabbi in Lemberg; he is buried near his two sons, Mordechai and Shlomo, who were both killed in a pogrom three years before his death. Rav Yehoshua Falk, the author of the Sm"a, who served as rav in Lemberg, and Rav Yaakov Meshulam Orenstein, the author of Yeshuos Yaakov, are also buried there.

After davening at the graves of these great individuals, the group came across a tombstone that seemed unusual and cryptic. It stated the person's name, followed by two words: "tzaddik nistar — hidden righteous person." Intrigued by their findings, the men approached the watchman of the cemetery and asked if he knew anything about this individual. Although he did not, he directed them to the city ledger, which contained information about those who were buried in the cemetery. They retrieved the ledger and leafed through it.

When they came to this grave, they discovered an interesting story.

ANY YEARS AGO, THE RAV OF THE CITY OF LEMBERG was known as a *heilege Yid*, a holy Jew. He was a *parush*, one who abstains from materialism. It was his normal practice to fast the entire week and eat only a bite each night.

One time, as he was on his way to shul on Friday evening before Shabbos, he felt a tap on his shoulder. When he turned around, he saw one of the simpletons of the community standing before him. The fellow asked the rav if he had fasted that day. Before he had a chance to answer the question, the fellow continued. "I know that you fasted today, but I also fasted today."

The rav thought that the exchange was a bit unusual but continued walking toward shul. However, the simpleminded man continued to escort the rav. A few minutes later, he piped up and asked another question. "How about yesterday? Did you fast yesterday, too?" Once more, before the rav had a chance to respond, the man added, "I also fasted yesterday."

The rav could not imagine what this fellow wanted, but the man was not finished. "How about the entire week? Did you fast the entire week? Because I also fasted the entire week. There's only one difference between the rav and me. You are going to sit down at your Shabbos table and eat a delicious meal of challah, fish, soup, and chicken. In this manner, you will revive yourself for the next week. But I am so poor that I just sit down with a piece of bread and salt, and that is how I break my fast."

The rav did not know who this man was, nor did he know what he was getting at, but he began to listen a bit more closely to what he was saying. "But just remember: When you get to your meal and they don't bring you the fish because the cat ate it, don't get angry. Because no amount of fasts or self-affliction will compensate for one's anger." By now, it was apparent that this simple fellow was not so simple after all. Although the rav was not sure what the fellow meant, he had a feeling that he would find out soon.

Following *Maariv* that evening, the rav went home and began his Shabbos meal. After he made *Kiddush* and ate the challah, he waited for his family members to bring out the fish. After waiting longer than usual, he asked the reason for the delay. Someone came in from the kitchen and informed him that a cat had jumped into the house and eaten the fish. He didn't understand how such a thing had happened and was about to get the tiniest bit upset, but then he remembered what the fellow had told him before Shabbos.

At this point, he realized that the simple fellow was a hidden *tzaddik*. Immediately, he sent a messenger to the man's house to ask him to come to his home.

When the messenger arrived at the hidden *tzaddik*'s home and relayed the message from the rav, the man responded, "There is a rule that if a hidden *tzaddik* is discovered, then he must die. And therefore, the time has come. What a shame that the rav did not come here himself. Had he come, I would have been able to reveal some of the greatest secrets of the Torah. But now it is too late."

The messenger ran back to the rav's home with the hidden *tzaddik*'s response. Upon hearing what was said, the rav ran to the *tzaddik*'s home to see if he could still speak to him. But by the time he reached the man's home, he had already left this world.

The rav informed the *chevrah kaddisha* of the man's death and all that had transpired that evening. He then told his family about his conversation with the deceased.

He concluded, "It was worthwhile for the simple man to reveal himself as a *tzaddik* and then be forced to leave this world before he had to, just to prevent me from getting angry.

"Because even a trace of anger can cause terrible destruction."

A MISSED CALL

ONE NIGHT AT 11:30, AFTER MAKING HIS ROUNDS FOR *bikur cholim,* Reb Boruch Medan was getting ready to leave the hospital. Suddenly, a nurse came running over to him and told him that a lonely man in the intensive care unit wanted to speak to a rabbi urgently. Although he hadn't been home all day and he was utterly exhausted, he agreed to visit the man. As it would turn out, these would be this individual's last moments on This Earth.

Reb Boruch walked into the intensive care unit and was directed to an older man, who seemed to be gasping for breath. Reb Boruch sat down next to him and asked him if there was anyone he wanted him to call. With an agitated look on his face, the patient insisted that he had no one and nothing left in This World. "I have no wife, no children, and no one to call."

But after a few moments, the man calmed down. Once again, Reb Boruch asked him if there was anyone he wanted him to reach out to. The fellow began to cry. "Yes, I have one son. My Dovid. I love him so much. *Oy!* My Dovid. . ."

My wife and I were married for a short while when our beautiful little Dovid was born. What an angelic child. He did everything right and everyone loved him. He was brilliant and soft spoken. Already at a very young age, he showed signs that he was destined for greatness. He finished many masechtos of Mishnayos and mastered each of them. When he began learning Gemara, he grasped the material very well.

My wife loved Dovid so much and did everything she could to enhance his learning. She would bake special treats to encourage him to learn more. She would make him hot chocolate, which he loved. There was nothing more important in the world to her.

Dovid was not satisfied with studying just the tractate he was learning in school, so we started to learn Sanhedrin together. The perek we chose was Dinei Mamonos Bi'Sheloshah.

That is what we were learning one day when the phone rang. It was the doctor. My wife had not been feeling well, and she had gone earlier that week to take some tests. Now he was calling with the results. When my wife answered the phone, her face went white. We ran to the doctor and he told us about the grim prognosis: my wife was sick and she was going to die. A few weeks later, she was taken to the hospital, and she asked Dovid to daven for her. When he asked her if she would be coming back, she promised she would. And she did come back. But it was for her funeral.

From that moment on, everything changed. At the funeral, Dovid was merely going through the motions. The world in which he had lived — the world he had loved — was gone.

Dovid stopped learning and stopped smiling. He even cut school. When confronted, he promised me he would go the next day. But when I called the school, he wasn't there. When he came home later that day, I asked him how he could have lied to me. He lashed out at me, "Why can't I lie? Imma lied to me. She promised me she would come home and she never did."

Within a few years, he was completely off the derech. He didn't keep Shabbos and didn't keep kosher. Eventually, he moved to America and married a non-Jew. They had six children. Can you imagine? Six grandchildren and they're not even Jewish! He knew how disappointed I was, but he didn't care at all.

He loved his new life and became very successful in business. He tried to speak to me every so often, but our

relationship became cold and barely cordial, until it disinte-
grated completely.

At this point, the elderly man seemed to slip into a reverie, as he repeated those three words, the words he had learned with his son before their lives turned upside down: "*Dinei Mamonus Bi'Sheloshah.*" Then he whispered, "How sweet it was. How sweet he was. My Dovid!"

Seeing how desperately ill the man was, Reb Boruch asked him, "Is there anything I can do for you? Do you want to daven? Do you want to say *Viduy*?"

But the elderly man shook his head vigorously. "No, I just want to talk to my Dovid."

Reb Boruch pulled out his cell phone and asked the old man for his son's telephone number. "I have not spoken to him in years, but I think that this is the number." He gave him the number and Reb Boruch dialed, as he whispered a small prayer that Dovid would pick up the phone.

Back in the United States, Dovid was in a jewelry store. His anniversary was coming up, and he wanted to buy something special for his wife. He was looking at different pieces of jewelry in the display case when his cell phone rang. He looked at it, and he saw that the call was coming from Israel. He figured it was his father, but this was not the right time to try to pick up the pieces of their fragmented relationship. He simply clicked the ignore button on his phone, and continued to peruse the jewelry.

At the hospital, as Reb Boruch held the cell phone to his ear, he heard it ringing but there was no answer. The man asked him to dial the number again. Midway through the exchange, there was silence in the room. The broken old man had breathed his last. Now Reb Boruch had no choice but to get hold of the man's son. When he finally got through, he said, "Hello. Is this Dovid? I am calling to tell you that your father just passed away."

Dovid was stunned. "How did you get my number?" he asked.

Reb Boruch told him that he was with his father, and he had tried to call just a few minutes earlier. "You should know," he explained, "that in the last few minutes of his life, he didn't want to pray and he didn't even want to say *Viduy*. All he wanted was to speak to you. He kept crying out your name."

Dovid was silent as the tears flowed freely. Along with the tears he was shedding for his father, he now shed the tears he had never shed for his mother.

Dovid arrived in Israel a short while later, just in time for the funeral. He didn't say a word. He just cried and cried over his father's grave. Although he did not know the man at all, except for the last moments of his life, Reb Boruch had helped with the arrangements for the funeral and made sure to attend. Upon seeing the nonreligious fellow crying over his father's grave, Reb Boruch immediately realized who he was. Reb Boruch approached him and introduced himself. As he wiped at his tears, Dovid asked, "Are there any other details you could share about my father's last moments on Earth?"

"Yes," said Reb Boruch. "Your father was singing in the sweetest tune, the three words that he learned with you when you were a little boy: '*Dinei Mamonos Bi'Sheloshah*.'" Upon hearing those three words, the words from a lifetime ago, Dovid burst out crying once more, and he began singing those same words.

He reached into his pocket and pulled out a piece of jewelry, the piece he had bought for his wife, instead of speaking to his father one last time. He looked at it with loathing. If only he had known. If only.

Many years had passed since the day that his mother died, and he had given up on a Torah life. His father had tried to bring him back — even at the last moment of his life.

If only he had known. If only he had known, he would have picked up the phone. But now it was too late.

WHAT REALLY MATTERS

Y ISRAEL YITZCHAK, THE YOUNGEST SON OF RAV BINYA-
min Mendelsohn, the well-known rav of Moshav Kome-
miyus, was beloved in the eyes of all members of the
community. With a charming personality and a smile that lit up
the room, he was almost like the mascot of the moshav. Whoever came to visit the moshav would somehow meet up with the
friendly youngster and take a liking to him.

Every two weeks, a truckload of ingredients arrived at the local
bakery. The ingredients were brought before the rav for inspec-
tion, to make sure that everything was up to his standards. On
one of those days, the driver of the truck noticed Yisrael Yitzchak
standing outside his house. While waiting for the ingredients to
be inspected, the driver offered the young man a ride. Yisrael
Yitzchak, who always enjoyed a good time and was looking for
some activity, hopped into the truck with the driver. After a few
moments, sensing that the young man was one who appreciated adventure, the 20-year-old driver offered him a turn at the
wheel.

Yisrael Yitzchak could hardly believe his good fortune.
Although it was an opportunity to drive just a few feet, it was
his first chance at the wheel and he jumped at it. After all, how
often does an 11-year-old boy get a chance to drive? Two weeks
later, the opportunity presented itself again. This time, he drove
a few hundred feet. The dangerous game expanded and before
long, the young man was driving around the fairly empty roads
of the moshav. He looked forward to these opportunities and relished the adventure. One day, the driver offered the now relatively
experienced 11-year-old an opportunity to take the truck onto the
highway that led to Be'er Sheva. Although the highways were not

as congested in the early 1970's as they are today, it was still an extremely dangerous venture.

But nothing seemed to faze Yisrael Yitzchak. Without hesitation, he began driving on the road. When he came to a traffic light, he noticed, to his chagrin, that the person in the car next to the truck was none other than his principal. At first, the principal did not recognize the young driver, but he looked again and immediately jumped out of his car. He opened Yisrael Yitzchak's door and pulled him out of the truck. He stared down the driver sitting next to Yisrael Yitzchak, and instructed him to bring the truck back to the moshav immediately. Yisrael Yitzchak understood that his adventure had come to a halt. Within a few moments, the three of them were back at Rav Mendelsohn's home. The principal walked into the house and spoke to the rav.

A few minutes later, he walked out and drove away. Not much needed to be said. With great trepidation, the boy waited outside his father's office, trembling at the thought of the punishment that awaited him. It wasn't until later that evening that his father called him in. When Yisrael Yitzchak entered the office, his father told him to sit down.

"Yisrael Yitzchak, I am very disappointed in your behavior. I already spoke to the driver, and I got the whole story from him. He is certainly at fault, too, but what you did was extremely dangerous. You risked the lives of many people just because you wanted to have a good time. You were careless and irresponsible. I want you to promise that you will never, ever do anything like that again."

Yisrael Yitzchak braced himself, still expecting a harsh punishment. But after he promised his father that he would never commit such a reckless act again, and that he would not drive before he got his license, his father no longer seemed angry and he did not punish him. He just instructed his son to go to sleep because it was late.

Yisrael Yitzchak's palms were sweaty and his heart was beating rapidly. However, after realizing that he was not going to be punished, he breathed a heavy sigh of relief. The next time the driver came, Yisrael Yitzchak kept his distance. Before long, the matter was forgotten. Yisrael Yitzchak seemed to have matured from the incident and began to focus his energy on his learning, in which he made tremendous strides over the next few months.

One day, a festive atmosphere filled the moshav. They were expecting a very special guest from America. The rosh yeshivah, Rav Yaakov Kamenetsky, was coming to visit, in order to view first-hand how the residents observed the laws of *Shemittah,* and to see the miraculous results they had experienced as a result of their observance.

While he was there, Rav Yaakov took the time to visit the school, speak to the boys, and administer a *bechinah* (test). Among the classes he visited was Yisrael Yitzchak's. With Rav Mendelsohn sitting at his side, Rav Yaakov asked the boys various questions. Yisrael Yitzchak answered every one of the questions posed to him perfectly, with clarity and confidence. He felt good about his answers and was proud that his father would also get some *nachas*.

That evening, his father called him into his office. Yisrael Yitzchak was certain that his father was going to compliment him on his excellent performance. Yet when he walked in, he saw that his father had a very angry look on his face. He thought about the last time that his father had called him into the office, when he had taken the truck for a pleasure ride. He remembered how nervous he was then, and that sentiment returned. His palms were sweaty and his heart was beating quickly.

Rav Mendelson began to speak. "You really gave me *nachas* today when you answered so beautifully in class. Hashem should help you to continue to learn so well."

Suddenly, his father began to cry. "But you also caused me tremendous pain, and for that I'm going to have to give you a punishment."

Yisrael Yitzchak was shocked. He had been on his best behavior and had answered all the questions perfectly. What could his father be upset about?

"After you answered your questions," explained his father, "the boy sitting next to you was asked some questions. When he stammered and stumbled over the answers, I saw that you were giggling. You laughed at another boy and embarrassed him further. There's nothing in the world that could cause me greater disappointment than that. How could you have done that to him? And because of this, I'm going to have to give you a *potch*."

The rav stood up, approached his son, and closed his eyes in concentration as if he were about to perform a mitzvah. With tears streaming down his face, for the first and only time in his child's life, he gave him a light *potch*.

A few years later, Yisrael Yitzchak, who had already blossomed into an exceptional young man, said to his father, "Please tell me the difference between the two cases. When I was driving the truck, all you did was reprimand me. But when I laughed at the other boy, you gave me a smack. Why? When I was driving on the road, I endangered other people's lives. I would think that I was more deserving of a punishment then."

"I will tell you the reason," replied the rav. "Driving the truck was truly a dangerous act. Therefore, I made you promise that you would never do it again. But that was wildness, and a child outgrows his wild tendencies. However, when you laughed at the other boy, that was a sign of a boy with bad *middos* at his core, which needed to be uprooted. If not, those bad character traits could have grown inside of you. That is why I had to punish you."

Yisrael Yitzchak grew into a *talmid chacham* of note and a genuine *baal middos*.

THE MEASURE
OF GREATNESS

I N PREWAR EUROPE, THERE WERE TWO MAIN APPROACHES
regarding the proper conduct and outlook of a *yeshivah bachur.*
One was the style of Novaradok. The network of the Novaradok yeshivos was established by the Alter of Novaradok, Rav Yosef
Yoizel Horowitz. He stressed the importance of *mussar* and taught
the boys the concept of *katnus ha'adam,* the smallness of man. To
this end, Novaradokers employed various means of deliberately
humiliating themselves — such as asking for screws in bakeries
— hoping to elicit a scathing rebuke. Their approach enhanced
their ability to grow without worrying about what others felt about
them. Their shabby clothing and indigent appearance enabled
them to fulfill their desire to find their proper place in this world.
The Steipler Gaon, Rav Yaakov Yisrael Kanievsky, was one product
of this movement.

The Slabodka Yeshivah stressed the opposite approach.
Founded by Rav Nosson Tzvi Finkel, known as the Alter of Slabodka, who was a student of Rav Simchah Zissel Ziv, the Alter
of Kelm, the yeshivah produced many of the leaders of the previous generation, including Rav Yitzchak Hutner, Rav Yaakov
Kamenetsky, Rav Aharon Kotler, and Rav Yaakov Yitzchak Ruderman. The Alter of Slabodka held that if man hopes to achieve his
goals, he must believe in his own greatness, in *gadlus ha'adam.*

Although the two approaches were vastly different, each produced Torah scholars and disseminated Torah to the masses in a
manner that resulted in a tremendous *kiddush Hashem.*

Eager to learn more about the concept of *gadlus ha'adam,* a
talmid of Yeshivas Chevron approached his mashgiach, Rav Meir

Chodosh. As a product of the Slabodka Yeshivah, Rav Meir had experienced the epitome of this ideology.

Rav Meir felt that if his *talmid* truly wanted to learn about *gadlus ha'adam,* he should spend some time in the company of Rav Zevulun Groz, the *av beis din* of Rechovot, who had also learned in Slabodka and exemplified the mantra and message of *gadlus ha'adam.*

The young man went to Rav Zevulun's home. He knocked on the door and asked the rav if he could spend the night there. Rav Zevulun happily agreed to host him and invited him in. He showed him to a room and prepared his bed for the evening.

The fellow did not plan on going to sleep that night, until he found his answer regarding *gadlus ha'adam.* As he lay in his bed fully awake, the hours passed and still he had not made any discoveries. Suddenly, at 2 a.m., he heard movement. He peeked out of his room and watched as the elderly man walked in his bathrobe toward the restroom. Not wanting to invade his privacy, he continued to wait until Rav Zevulun emerged.

However, instead of going back to his room, Rav Zevulun walked toward the closet. He opened the door, took out his long jacket, and put it on over his robe. Then he reached for his hat and put it on his head. With his jacket buttoned and his hat in place, he closed his eyes. With great concentration, he recited the blessing of *Asher Yatzar.* After he finished, he removed his hat and jacket and put them back in the closet.

The young man had found what he was looking for. He came seeking the greatness of man, and witnessed just that. He did not see it by watching someone grandstand in front of an audience of thousands. That is not where one finds true greatness. True greatness is found when no one else is around.

SWEAT THE SMALL STUFF

RAV MORDECHAI ZEV BLAU, A CLOSE *TALMID* OF THE Munkatcher Rebbe, the Minchas Elazar, was traveling with the Rebbe by train. A man sitting near them took out a ham sandwich. He had just pulled off a piece and was ready to put it into his mouth, when the Rebbe cried out, "Jew, it is forbidden to eat ham!" The traveler calmly replied, "I am not a Jew, so it is completely permissible for me to eat my sandwich. Please don't bother me."

Once again, the fellow was about to put the piece of the sandwich into his mouth when the Rebbe cried out, "Jew, it is forbidden to eat ham!" By now, the fellow was losing his patience. He looked determinedly at the Rebbe and insisted, "I told you once and I'll tell you again. I am not a Jew and I am allowed to eat my sandwich. Please leave me alone!"

But the Rebbe would not relent. He begged the fellow not to eat the sandwich. Finally, the man took his sandwich, stood up, and walked to the window of the train. After a few moments, he opened the window and threw out the sandwich. When he looked back at the Rebbe, his eyes were red and filled with tears. "Rabbi," he said, "I have met hundreds of people over the years. None of them ever suspected that I am a Jew; I conceal it well. How did you know?"

The Rebbe took his hand and held it. "I saw how you were going to eat your sandwich, and through that I was able to tell that you are a Jew. There is a law in the *Shulchan Aruch* [*Orach Chaim* 170:10,15] regarding biting out of a piece of bread and leaving it on the table or giving it to one's friend. The sight of a slice of bread with bite marks is repulsive to those who see it. As such, Jewish people have the custom to pull off pieces of the bread, instead of biting into the whole slice or sandwich. When I saw you doing that, I presumed it was because your parents taught you to eat the sandwich in this manner."

The fellow listened carefully and smiled. Indeed, he had grown up in a religious home, but had been faced by many challenges early on in life. Before long, he found himself committing all types of sins, until the point where he was able to eat pig meat.

This encounter with the Rebbe ignited a spark inside the man. Instead of continuing toward his intended destination, he traveled with the Rebbe. In a matter of weeks, he became a complete *baal teshuvah* and one of the closest disciples of the Rebbe.

Interestingly, that was not the last time Rav Mordechai Zev witnessed the power of this halachah.

After the war, as he and others went searching for Jewish children hidden in Christian monasteries and orphanages, Rav Mordechai Zev was informed by the clergyman in one particular institution that there were no Jewish children there. Not trusting the priest, the rav walked into the dining room and began observing the children as they were eating sandwiches. One boy named Josef cut his sandwich as he ate it, so Rav Mordechai Zev asked the boy where he had learned to cut his sandwich in that manner. The boys was quiet, unable to respond since the priest was standing right there. After a few moments, the child began to cry. He ran over to Rav Mordechai Zev and told him that he was a Jew.

By inculcating in our children these small but important customs, it can make an everlasting impression on them. One Chol HaMoed, as Rav Yitzchak Silverstein related these two stories at a gathering, a distinguished lawyer asked for permission to speak.

He said that he had met with a very wealthy individual that

morning in order to sign on a very big business deal. However, the lawyer told Rav Silverstein, he had refused to sign until after Yom Tov. And then he explained:

> I only did this because of my parents who were killed in the Holocaust. My father was a simple carpenter, and we had very little money. When Chol HaMoed came, my father surmised that he was allowed to work, since there is an allowance for one who is a "po'el she'ein lo mah le'echol — a worker who does not have what to eat" [Orach Chaim 542:2]. However, I remember that my mother asked my father not to work. She said that even though he was technically allowed to work because we didn't have any money, it would be worthwhile for us to rely on Hashem and to show Him that we love Him, and that we love to perform His mitzvos. And we would not lose out. In the end, my father agreed and did not work on Chol HaMoed.
>
> I was a young boy at the time, but I heard the entire discussion and the message was not lost on me. My mother's commitment and my father's willingness not to work took tremendous sacrifice. They chose to forgo that day's profits and instead to rely on the Al-mighty. All of that made a tremendous impression on me.

"This morning as I was about to sign," continued the lawyer, "I thought of my parents. I thought about their sacrifice and I realized that it would be proper for me not to finalize the deal, and to put my trust in Hashem. If the other party decides not to go through with the deal, then so be it. I will have no regrets."

> No detail is too small. Whether it is cutting a sandwich or adhering to the laws of Chol HaMoed, even if there is room for leniency, we must not minimize the impact our actions can have on our children's future.

OF OMELETS
AND EDUCATION

I N BNEI BRAK THERE IS A WELL-KNOWN *TALMID CHACHAM* named Rav Yudkovsky. On one occasion, he traveled to Tel Aviv and was looking for a place to daven *Minchah*. Eventually, he found a small shul. Before they began davening, the *gabbai* of the shul announced to the congregants that since their normal *maggid shiur* had not come that day, the *Mishnayos shiur* that usually took place between *Minchah* and *Maariv* was canceled.

When Rav Yudkovsky heard the announcement, he felt bad that these laymen — who looked forward to this class for their daily learning — would miss out, so he offered to teach the *Mishnayos* that day. The *gabbai* gladly agreed and distributed the *Mishnayos* as soon as *Minchah* was over.

The group was in the middle of *Seder Taharos,* up to a very difficult *perek*. Apparently, most of the people in the group did not comprehend the material, except for one person who asked many questions. His grasp of the complex concepts surprised Rav Yudkovsky. After *Maariv*, Rav Yudkovsky asked the man where he was from and how he knew how to learn so well.

The fellow told over his story, which carries a powerful message.

> *I was born in Golders Green, England. When I finished high school, I was the only one of my group of friends who wanted to learn Torah and not pursue higher secular education. I knew that the best place for me to learn Torah would be in Eretz Yisrael. Although my parents were hesitant at first, eventually they gave in and sent me off to learn.*

I began to look for a good yeshivah, one where I could maximize my potential. However, even though I really wanted to learn, my background was weak. I went from one yeshivah to the next, and I interviewed at all of them. None of the roshei yeshivah were willing to accept me. They were all very nice but they insisted that I spend some time in a preparatory school before coming back to them. Although they were right, I desperately wanted to be like everyone else and to learn in a regular yeshivah.

After a number of days and countless interviews, I began to lose hope. Finally, someone suggested that I try my luck with Rav Elyah Lopian, the mashgiach in Kfar Chassidim. I was told to prepare the first five blatt [folios] of Maseches Bei-tzah. It was down to earth and practical material; even though I didn't have much experience in learning, I would be able to understand it. I prepared very well and worked very hard.

After one week, I went to Rav Elyah's house and introduced myself. I told him how much I wanted to learn, and that I want to attend his yeshivah. I was as sincere as I had ever been and prayed in my heart that he would accept me.

Rav Elyah asked me what I had prepared, and I told him. He began to ask me questions on those folios, but I couldn't answer any of them. In my nervousness, I forgot everything I had learned. With each missed question, my mind went further and further blank. I was never so embarrassed in my life.

Rav Elyah picked up immediately on how I felt, and he reached out to me and held my hand. He tried to calm me down, as he asked me a very simple question: "What do you do with a beitzah she'noldah beYom Tov — an egg that is hatched on Yom Tov?"

By that point, all of the encouragement and calming in the world weren't going to help me. I couldn't think at all. I couldn't even remember the first words of the first Mishnah.

In my past experiences, I would have already been rejected. But Rav Elyah was not deterred. Again, he told me not to worry and repeated, "What is the halachah with a beitzah she'noldah be'Yom Tov?"

I tried to think, but I couldn't. Finally, after he asked me the question again very slowly, I responded, "If an egg was hatched on Yom Tov, you would use it to make an omelet." I knew that it was the most ridiculous answer anyone could have ever given, but it was all I could think of at that moment.

Imagine what would have happened if someone did that today. Obviously, he would have been rejected. The one administering the test would have berated him and told him that he was a mechutzaf [an impudent person].

However, that is not what happened to me. Rav Elyah understood what was going on inside of me. He saw that I wanted to learn. He saw that I had prepared the material. Otherwise, I would never have knocked on his door.

He told me, "Your answer is not correct. But I am still going to accept you into our yeshivah, because I see inside of you a great desire to learn. I also see that you think clearly. When you didn't know the answer, you said to yourself, 'What would someone do with an egg?' And you answered, of course, that he would make an omelet. Indeed, what else does one do with an egg?"

Those words lifted me and stoked my desire to become better and to continue to learn. After I enrolled, I began to see success in my learning, and I went flying through the system. Before long, I was considered one of the best boys in the yeshivah. By the time I left, I knew the tractates of Nashim and Nezikin with Rashi and Tosafos, inside out.

All because of Rav Elyah.

"After I got married," concluded the man, "my wife and I had 13 children. They weren't all brilliant from the start. However, I had learned how one must build a child. Now, all of them are *mar-bitzei Torah* [disseminators of Torah]."

Whether you are a teacher teaching your class, or a parent doing homework with your child, always remember that the point of the test is to see what the child knows, not what he does not know.

THE BLACK BOOK

RAV MENDEL KERVITZ IMMIGRATED TO ERETZ YISRAEL from Vilna. When he arrived, in the late 1940's, there was a shortage of food; poverty was rampant and disease lurked everywhere. The homes were decrepit and the people's clothes were worn out, yet happiness and joy ruled in the streets. It was a happiness borne of the knowledge that they were doing their *avodas Hashem* in spite of all the challenges.

Rav Mendel, who had to support his family of 10, began seeking a job, any position that could put some food on his table. His name was mentioned as a possible candidate as a *melamed* in a Talmud Torah. Upon meeting Rav Mendel, the *menahel* of the Talmud Torah quickly perceived Rav Mendel's refined soul, intelligent mind, and eyes that burned with fear of Heaven and love of fellow Jews. Without hesitation, he said to Rav Kervitz, "The job is yours."

Rav Mendel developed a reputation as an outstanding and caring rebbi. His students looked forward to his lessons. Long after they left his class, they maintained a relationship with him. He expected to keep his job as a *melamed* for the rest of his life. One day, however, the principal called him into his office and told him that he was planning to retire, and that he had chosen Rav Mendel as his successor.

Although he was hesitant to take the job, Rav Mendel discussed the proposal with a number of people whom he respected; they all felt that he would make an excellent principal. Though the task seemed daunting — he was going from being responsible for 25 children to being responsible for 300 — he prepared himself to undertake the challenge.

As *menahel*, Rav Kervitz ran an efficient school and was well respected among teachers and students alike. However, his trademark was his ubiquitous black book. He took it with him wherever he went. Throughout the day, he would jot down mysterious notes inside its pages.

When he walked into a classroom, he would listen for a few moments and then record something in his black book. When he stood in the playground during recess, he looked around and watched the boys play. Afterward, he took out his black book and wrote down his observations. When he walked around the dining room at lunchtime, he observed the boys eating. Then, once again, he would take out his black book and mark down his thoughts.

Although they respected their principal, the boys were annoyed that he was always writing down notes in his ever-present black book. They were sure that he was noting who didn't know the material, who was misbehaving at recess, and who was not eating with proper manners in the dining room.

One day, a group of boys approached Rav Mendel's 11-year-old son Eliezer and asked him to sneak a peek into the black book. But Eliezer wouldn't hear of it. He could never break his father's trust. Although he himself didn't care that much for the black book, he fully trusted his father. He assumed that his father was writing down notes that pertained to the children's education.

Late one night, Eliezer noticed his father's coat hanging over a chair. On the kitchen table, open for all to see, was the black book! He thought of all the times that his friends had asked him to take a peek, and he was tempted to do so. But he dismissed the thought. Yet, as time passed, he couldn't overcome his curiosity. Thus, when he was sure no one was around — though he felt terribly guilty — he peeked.

He could not believe what he was reading:

"At recess today, I noticed that Dovid Schwartz was wearing torn pants. I must make sure to find a way to get him new ones. Eli Frisch in fifth grade did not have a well-prepared lunch. I must find out if everything is okay at home, and I need to bring a lunch for him. Mordechai Katzenberg has holes in his shoes. I will have to speak to Mr. Mandelbaum to see if he can buy him a new pair."

The list went on and on. There was not one bad word written in the "dreaded" black book.

There were comments about the rebbeim, as well. The second-grade rebbi was making a bar mitzvah and could use some assistance. The sixth-grade rebbi was suffering from monetary challenges and needed a loan. And so on.

Eliezer wished he could tell his friends that they were wrong about his father. He wanted to tell them what an exceptional person his father was. However, he knew that his discovery had to be kept to himself.

Years later, after Rav Mendel Kervitz passed away, the rest of the family discovered what Eliezer already knew. Dozens of black books were found, each one filled with lists of people Rav Mendel had helped.

While on the topic of devoted principals, here is another story that shows us the meaning of true dedication — to Hashem and to His children.

Mrs. Beverly Koval grew up in Cleveland, Ohio. Her parents were simple, good Yidden who survived the Holocaust and retained their rock-solid *emunah* even after all they had gone through. When their daughters were young, they made the decision to send

Beverly and her only sibling to the fledgling Hebrew Academy of Cleveland (HAC). Beverly flourished at HAC and developed a life-long love of learning, along with the desire to keep coming closer to Hashem.

After she got married, raised eight children who attended HAC, and headed the PTA for many years, she was offered the job as principal of the Girls Elementary School of the HAC. She accepted the job and excelled in this role as a *mashpia* (woman of influence) on the lives of young *bnos Yisrael* (Jewish daughters), until her passing 14 years later.

Mrs. Koval lived by the *pasuk*, "*Ve'habotei'ach baHashem, chesed yesovevenu* — But as for one who trusts in Hashem, kindness surrounds him" (*Tehillim* 32:10). This became most obvious after her death, when her family found a note inside her desk, which she had written on the first day at her job as principal.

> *Today they cleared out the office assigned to me. They are calling me principal, a title that fills me with sadness and shame. I don't know if I deserve that title. The position carries with it an obligation. May it be Your will, Hashem, that I succeed in Your work, for the sake of Your service and Your glory.*
>
> *I must make decisions about when to discipline and when to grant pardon to the girls, conduct discussions with teachers, etc. . . I am filled with a simple prayer: May it be Your will that I speak and act intelligently and may the merit of the many stand on my behalf, as I personally don't have the reserves for the burdens placed upon me.*
>
> *Today was a very hard and busy day. Perhaps I demanded too much, but You, Master of the Universe, know that I did nothing and do nothing except for the needs of the precious girls knocking at our doors.*

Years later, Mrs. Koval's memory and the lessons she epitomized are still reflected upon by the teachers at HAC; they think about her and her greatness whenever they need a boost of clarity and guidance.

For all that she did was for the sake of His service and His glory.

THE POWER OF A COMPLIMENT

A compliment has the power to change people's lives in an instant. It can give them a boost and transform the way they look at themselves, and the way they look at life.

I once took a young man to Rav Shalom Kamenetsky, a rosh yeshivah in Talmudical Yeshiva of Philadelphia. The boy needed a little pick-me-up. Rav Shalom cited the pasuk in Mishlei (27:2): "Yehalelcha zar ve'lo ficha — Let another praise you, not your own mouth." Simply understood, this means that a person should not praise himself, but leave the compliments to others.

But the Vilna Gaon has a different explanation: "Yehalelcha zar — Let another praise you;" however, "ve'lo — if not," then: "ficha — you should praise yourself." A person must be able to look in the mirror and feel good about himself. He must know his talents and his abilities.

About 100 years ago, Yaakov, a curious child, noticed a grandfather clock in his dining room. The boy reached for the clock and began to examine it closely, but he was not satisfied. Then he opened the large clock from the back and took it apart. When his mother walked into the room and saw what her son had done, she reprimanded him. "What did you do? How will your father know when he has to go learn? How will we know when Shabbos is?"

The child was startled by the rebuke. Just then, his father walked into the room. Sizing up the situation, he told his wife that there is another way to view Yaakov's act. "Don't you see? Our child is bright and inquisitive. He is not satisfied until he discovers how the grandfather clock works. This is how he's going to learn Torah, too. Perhaps he will grow up to be a *talmid chacham,* and he will show his students how to delve into a *sugya* [topic], as well."

Yaakov fulfilled his father's hopes and dreams. Yet even after he became the great Rav Yaakov Yitzchak Ruderman, the rosh yeshivah of Ner Yisroel, he always held this story close to his heart.

His father had found a way to validate his inquisitiveness, and that meant the world to him.

When Rav Isser Zalman Meltzer arrived in Eretz Yisrael, one of the first people he visited was Rav Zelig Reuven Bengis, the rav of the Eidah HaChareidis of Yerushalayim. He told Rav Bengis that all he accomplished in his life — he authored *sefarim,* he was a rosh yeshivah, he had prestigious children — was because of him. Rav Bengis was surprised. He was only vaguely connected to Rav Isser Zalman at the time. How could he have been the catalyst for his success?

Rav Isser Zalman recounted that when he first came to Yeshivas Volozhin, he had so many patches on his clothing that the patches far outweighed the rest of the fabric. He was so embarrassed by his appearance that he was ready to go back home. Then he met with the rosh yeshivah, the Netziv, Rav Naftali Tzvi Yehudah Berlin, and spoke with him in learning. During the course of this discussion, the Netziv asked Isser Zalman a question and was astonished by his brilliant answer.

When the Netziv came out of the room, he remarked to Zelig Reuven Bengis, who was an older *bachur* at the time, how impressed he was with the young man's answer. Zelig Reuven looked for this boy who had so impressed the Netziv, and repeated the compliment to the young newcomer. This made Isser Zalman feel so good about himself that he no longer wanted to go home.

Years later, he still attributed his success to the person who had relayed the compliment.

When Yehudah, a 9-year-old boy who lived in Yerushalayim, heard that the Imrei Emes, Rav Avraham Mordechai Alter, was visiting his city, he wanted to get a *berachah*. Though there was a large crowd around the Rebbe, Yehudah managed to wiggle his way to the front of the line.

The Rebbe shook his hand and asked Yehudah what he was learning. The boy responded that he was learning *Maseches Shabbos*. Before blessing him, the Imrei Emes asked him why there are 24 chapters in *Maseches Shabbos*. The boy had no idea, but he said that he would find out. He ran to a nearby shul, where he found Rav Yaakov Chaim Sofer, the author of the *Kaf HaChaim,* learning in the *beis midrash*, and he posed the question to him.

Rav Sofer gave him two answers. First of all, Shabbos is compared to a bride, and the *navi* Yeshayah says that a bride is adorned with 24 adornments. These correspond to the 24 chapters of *Shabbos*. Also, the 24 chapters correspond to the 24 books of the *Tanach,* since when one keeps Shabbos, it is considered as if he has kept the entire Torah.

Yehudah ran back to the Rebbe with his response. Impressed with the young man, the Rebbe gave him a gift, a five-*gerush* coin. The boy ran home to share the wonderful news with his mother. As a niece of the Ben Ish Chai, she knew the true value of Torah;

she treasured the gift her son had received. She punched a hole in it and created a necklace for Yehudah to wear at all times.

Yehudah blossomed into Rav Yehudah Tzadka, the rosh yeshivah of Porat Yosef, and a teacher to thousands. Years later, the coin was misplaced but its lesson remained. It reminded Rav Tzadka that a great man appreciated the trouble a young boy went through to come back with an answer, and of the warm feeling that boy carried around with him as a result.

Never underestimate the power of a compliment.

IT STARTS WITH A CUP OF COFFEE

FROM 1930 UNTIL 1942, RAV ELIYAHU PARDES RAN A GIRLS' school in the Ohel Moshe neighborhood in Yerushalayim. He undertook this job with a tremendous sense of responsibility, devoting his time and energy to the *chinuch* of the girls; his dedication and commitment were well known. He never looked to cut corners. No detail was too minor, as he was always ready to address every problem head-on. The students and teachers all knew that he was there for them, 100 percent.

Even so, there was one part of his day that was more important than the school. Everyone who was acquainted with him knew that for one hour in the morning, he was unavailable. For that was the time he spent with his elderly father. Each and every morning, he would come to his father's house, prepare a cup of coffee for his father and for himself, and then sit down with his father. They would both enjoy their coffee, along with some biscuits. Rav Eliyahu and his father would discuss whatever his father wanted to talk about. Come what may, this meeting was sacred.

However, one time Rav Eliyahu forgot all about this meeting. It was a very busy morning indeed. Sir Herbert Samuel, the first viscount of Palestine, was invited to the school and would be visiting for the morning. Sir Herbert was a very influential and powerful individual, and it was imperative that the students, teachers, and administrators make an excellent impression on him. There was no room for error.

For weeks beforehand, all the girls and staff members prepared. The students decorated signs welcoming Sir Herbert to the school. All the fixtures, desks, and other furniture that were broken were repaired, and the building was cleaned from top to bottom. Hence, by the time the auspicious morning dawned, the school had never looked better.

In honor of their illustrious visitor, the children had been asked to dress in their very best clothing, and to make sure that their hair was neat and their shoes polished. They were coached about proper behavior and etiquette in front of the famous personage. As the girls arrived on that morning, each of them felt the anticipation in the air. They stood at their desks and awaited instructions.

Their distinguished guest was scheduled to arrive at precisely 9 a.m. Rav Eliyahu knew that Sir Herbert was a stickler for punctuality, and he had every reason to assume that today would be no different.

Rav Eliyahu was pleased with the preparations. Nevertheless, he was nervous and eager for the meeting to be over. He was well aware that his students could not be on their best behavior forever.

It stands to reason that because of all the commotion surrounding this monumental event, Rav Eliyahu forgot about the most important meeting of all, about having coffee with his father. But anyone who knew the circumstances would never have blamed him for the oversight.

It was two minutes before 9 o'clock, and Sir Herbert was just about to arrive. Suddenly, a bent-over figure appeared at the school. The elderly fellow, who was wearing a cap and a sports jacket, slowly made his way up the steps of the front entrance of the school building. Those who were standing there were somewhat surprised. He did not appear to be the man they were expecting.

Rav Eliyahu was called to the entrance. When he saw the visitor, he nearly fainted. It was none other than his father. It suddenly dawned on him that he had forgotten all about their daily meeting.

"Abba!" he called as he ran up to his father and asked him why he had come. His father replied, "When you didn't come to visit me today, I was concerned. I wanted to make sure that nothing happened to you. I am so happy to see that you are feeling fine and everything is all right. But tell me: Why didn't you come this morning?"

Rav Eliyahu felt like crying. How could he have forgotten? Racked with feelings of guilt, he decided to make things right. He turned to his assistant and told him that he had to leave. The assistant blanched; he was not sure how he would manage on his own at this critical visit. He did not want to be disrespectful, but he had no idea what could possibly be more important than meeting the viscount.

Rav Eliyahu reassured his assistant: "Listen. There is no reason to worry. We prepared for this for weeks. I am sure you will do a great job in welcoming Sir Herbert. However, I must go and take care of something extremely important."

And just like that, Rav Eliyahu turned around, took his father's hand, and walked him out of the building. The assistant and the rest of the people standing there could not believe what they had just witnessed. This was, without question, the most important meeting they would ever have with a government official. And now, their principal had walked out on them moments before his arrival. But they knew not to question. If there was anyone who was fair and just, it was Rav Eliyahu. In fact, he was right; they were well prepared and there was no reason for concern or worry.

What a lesson he had taught them. His elderly father and their simple cup of coffee were more important than anything else in the world, even Sir Herbert Samuel.

Rav Eliyahu walked his father back to his house and they had their coffee. He did not rush him, nor did he even tell him exactly why he had forgotten. He just said that there was a lot going on at the school, and he apologized for the oversight. He did not want his father to feel bad or to feel pressured to end their morning coffee before the regular time.

After spending time with his father, he apologized once more for forgetting and made his way back to the school. By the time he arrived, the visit was nearly over. He walked over to Sir Herbert and introduced himself as the headmaster of the school. The assistant principal had told the viscount that the headmaster had an urgent matter to attend to. Now that Rav Eliyahu had finally shown up, the viscount wanted to know: What could be more pressing than a visit with an important government official? Not that Sir Herbert was a haughty individual, but he knew that this meeting was essential for the school.

Rav Eliyahu sensed that the viscount was a bit agitated, so he told him the truth. "Your honor, every single morning I have coffee and breakfast with my elderly father. My mother died many years ago, and he is very lonely. I was so consumed with the preparations for your arrival that I simply forgot about visiting my father. Right before you arrived, however, he came to the school looking for me. I felt that the correct action at that moment was to make up for my mistake and join him, albeit a bit later than usual. So I left and went to have coffee with my father as I always do. I apologize profusely if you were slighted, but I did what I felt had to be done."

The viscount of Palestine, the most prominent British Jew living at that time, looked at Rav Eliyahu with great admiration. Then he smiled at the headmaster and gave him a warm hug. "Fortunate are the Jewish people, for they have individuals who treat their parents with such respect. I want you to know that I was quite impressed with the appearance of the school: how it is run so efficiently, and how well the children behave. But nothing impressed me as much as what you just told me. Indeed, the children of this school are very privileged to be able to learn from your example on a daily basis."

And with that, Sir Herbert Samuel took his leave, forever enriched by what he had just witnessed.

Unfortunately, there is no guidebook to teach us how to honor our parents as they grow older. Often it is challenging.

My father and his two brothers all had tremendous respect for their mother, Mrs. Elissa Spero – a regal woman who has been mentioned in my books – and treated her like a queen. Although she was a relatively independent woman for most of her life, my father always went to the library for her and brought her books he thought she would like. He would visit her almost daily and look after her needs.

The one time each week that was most treasured by my father and his brothers, as well as their mother, was Friday afternoon. At that time, though they were all grandfathers by then, the three brothers would meet at their mother's house and have a cup of coffee with her.

After she passed away, they still wanted to get together for a cup of coffee, and so they would meet every Friday afternoon at a local coffee shop. But alas, it was not the same.

Indeed, the challenge of honoring one's parents becomes greater as they get older. But it starts with the basics.

It starts with a cup of coffee.

ACCEPTANCE NO MATTER WHAT

Regardless of the religious sect or circle, whenever the Chasam Sofer, Rav Moshe Schreiber, is mentioned, his name brings with it admiration and reverence. It is true that he was brilliant and righteous, but so were so many others. And so, the question must be asked: Why? Why did he merit a greater level of acceptance than many other gedolim?

When the Munkatcher Rebbe, the Minchas Elazar, was asked this question, he suggested that the veneration accorded the Chasam Sofer was due to the following episode.

THE YESHIVAH OF PRESSBURG CONSISTED OF 400 OF the finest Hungarian *bachurim,* who came to glean from the Chasam Sofer's style of teaching, as well as his depth and mastery of the *sugya* (topic).

The cycle of learning in the yeshivah took three years, though some *bachurim* stayed for longer. However, there was one brilliant young man, whose name was Landsberg, who stayed for a much longer time: for over nine years, or more than three full cycles. He knew the Chasam Sofer's *shiurim* backward and forward, as he had heard each one multiple times.

Now, with the onset of the fourth cycle and many new *bachurim* in attendance, he decided to have a good time at the expense of the Chasam Sofer.

Not only did Landsberg know everything that his rebbi was going to say, but he was also very talented at mimicking the motions and nuances of the Chasam Sofer. When many of the young men were already in the room in which the *shiur* was to be delivered, but the rebbi had not yet arrived, Landsberg began to give over the *shiur* verbatim. It was a masterful imitation, though exceedingly *chutzpahdik*. Many of the young men were uncomfortable with the presentation, but some laughed and enjoyed his clownlike imitation.

In due time, the Chasam Sofer arrived and began to deliver his *shiur*. As always, the *shiur* consisted of precisely the same thoughts he had conveyed three years earlier. He was not incapable of coming up with original thoughts, but he felt that these ideas were most effective in helping the young men develop their skills and understand the depth and intricacies of the discussion in the Gemara. This time, though, he noticed that many of the young men were smiling or snickering. At first, he ignored the unusual behavior, but when it continued, he asked a boy who was seated in the front what could possibly be so humorous.

The fellow told him that a *bachur* from the yeshivah had stood before the crowd right before the Chasam Sofer had arrived and had given the exact *shiur*, complete with all the nuances and hand motions.

The Chasam Sofer was appalled that somebody could behave in such a manner and declared, "If this is the way people treat the *shiur*, then I refuse to give it." And with that, to the shock and dismay of the nearly 400 *bachurim* who were present, he walked out.

Seconds later, a tumult erupted, the likes of which had never before been seen in Pressburg. Who could possibly imagine the punishment in store for such an individual who had made fun of the great Chasam Sofer, and caused him to get so upset?

The next day, the Chasam Sofer told the *gabbaim* to announce that he expected full attendance at that day's *shiur*. Anyone who did not show up would be asked to leave the yeshivah. This announcement came as no surprise. Everyone knew that the fellow who had imitated their rebbi deserved to suffer severe consequences. Publicly, if needed.

Sure enough, when the time for *shiur* arrived, every seat was filled. Sitting right in the front row was none other than Landsberg, the *mechutzaf* himself. He knew that he had stepped over the line — that even on Purim such behavior would have been considered reprehensible, though perhaps more easily understood — and that his actions were disgraceful. Bracing for the worst, he sat in his seat and trembled.

Finally, the Chasam Sofer arrived. He surveyed the room and looked at the nearly 400 young men who were sitting and waiting with bated breath, wondering what would happen. "*Bachurim*, we are all aware of what took place yesterday before I said my *shiur*. One young man, who is sitting right here, mimicked the manner in which I give *shiur*. I'm sure you also remember the way I reacted. I stormed out and made a sharp declaration about what a terrible misdeed had taken place."

He paused for a moment and then let out a scream that would never be forgotten: "*Shame on me!*

"How could I have embarrassed one of my *talmidim* in such a manner? I had no right to disgrace him in public. That is why I asked everybody to come today as I ask him publicly for forgiveness, and I promise that I will never behave like that again."

The Chasam Sofer stood up and walked out of the room. The room was dead silent, the *bachurim* awestruck by the humility and *vatranus* [the act of giving in] they had just witnessed.
Of course, Landsberg went over and begged the Chasam Sofer for forgiveness. He cried for a long time, truly anguished that he had displayed such poor judgment.

When the Minchas Elazar finished relaying this incident, he explained, "If we wonder why the heilige [holy] Chasam Sofer is more widely accepted than anyone else, it is because of the way he treated his students. He accepted them and their behavior — no matter what — even when someone committed a gross injustice against him. Whereas many other figures of authority would have banished the impudent and rebellious young man from entering the yeshivah again, the Chasam Sofer turned the tables; he was the one who asked for forgiveness.

What a lesson! We must accept our students with all of their faults and shortcomings. We must embrace them and love them and do whatever we can to help them. If we feel that we have wronged them, we must humbly ask mechilah (forgiveness).

In addition, if there is ever a need to ask a young man to leave a school, we cannot just let go of him. We must hold onto him and follow his progress, checking in constantly and letting him know that we care deeply about him and his future.

If we are willing to follow the example of the Chasam Sofer, maybe, just maybe, we will all be accepted back into the good graces of the Ribbono Shel Olam.

NECHAMAH

A MOTHER'S EMBRACE

The following story was told by Rav Yissachar Shlomo Teich-tal, the author of Eim HaBanim Semeichah.

I N 1942, PRIOR TO THE YOM TOV OF PESACH, THE SLOVAKIAN government issued a proclamation demanding that all girls 16 and older report to the authorities. When the order was ignored, Nazi guards rounded up thousands of young innocent girls, who were never heard from again.

When he heard the announcement, one Slovakian Jew, aware of the Nazis' plans, attempted to save his daughters by smuggling them across the border. It was Chol HaMoed Pesach — ironically, *z'man cheiruseinu* — when he carried out his plan. In a time destined for freedom, this family hoped that their exodus would turn out favorably, as well, as improbable as that seemed. The man packed some meager supplies, and he and his two daughters headed out in the stealth of the night. He promised his wife that as soon as they were safe, he would send her a telegram. The mother kissed her daughters goodbye and hugged them tightly. And then, just like that, they were gone.

The road was treacherous and the path was fraught with danger. With every step they took, they knew that they could be caught and then their lives would be over. Although they were extremely cautious and quiet, they were apprehended by local police and taken to prison. Even though this was better than being caught by the Nazi guards, they feared the worst.

The local authorities had taken them to a prison in a nearby city, not a place where young girls could feel safe. Their father did his utmost to protect them, as they sat there — alongside the lowlifes of Slovakian society. As long as they were in prison, the danger of being handed over to the Nazi authorities was very real and very frightening. If they were taken by the Nazis, they would be punished severely, and their fate could be far worse than if they had reported to the Nazis as instructed.

In the meantime, their wife and mother waited at home with bated breath, hoping to hear some good news. But with each passing day, her anxieties and worries grew. They should have sent word long ago of their safe arrival; the delay could only spell trouble. Finally, after a number of days, word reached her that her husband and daughters were incarcerated in a local prison. Her pain knew no bounds; she cried incessantly, as she imagined what her poor husband and daughters were going through. Although she tried to be hopeful, she was painfully aware of the strong possibility that she would never see her husband or her daughters again.

Rav Shmuel Dovid Ungar, better known as the Nitra Rav, was a leader of Slovakian Jewry. He invested every ounce of his energy to save as many Jews as possible, risking his life countless times. Rav Shmuel Dovid heard of the plight of the father and his daughters, and he left no stone unturned as he raised a large sum of money to bribe the local authorities to let them free.

It was on the last day of Yom Tov that the three captives were set free, and a telegram was sent to their wife and mother, informing her that, G-d willing, her husband and daughters would be arriving home the next day.

In Rav Yissachar Shlomo's words: "Who can imagine the expression of joy on the woman's face, and the feelings of gratitude in her heart, when she heard the joyous news that her husband and her children were freed from the jaws of almost certain death? From the time she heard the news, she waited and yearned for the moment that they would arrive home safely.

"She sat in her courtyard the next day, and her eyes did not leave its entrance. When they finally appeared, she cried tears of joy and relief, as she ran over to her daughters and held them. She was so overcome with emotion that she could barely get the words out as she expressed her gratitude to the Al-mighty for the incredible miracle that her family had experienced. Those who were present at the time, and saw the mother together with her family and heard the cries when she saw her children, stated that they had never seen such a display of joy."

Rav Yissachar Shlomo then delivered a meaningful message. After being in captivity for nearly 2,000 years, we will finally be redeemed. We will make our trek back to Eretz Yisrael, "our mother," who anticipates our arrival. When the moment comes, we will run into her arms and she will embrace us with love and affection.

And all who observe this reunion will say that they have never seen such joy.

MOVING FORWARD

THE SEVEN DAYS OF *SHIVAH* FOR RAV SHIMON SHALOM Kalish of Amshinov were now over. Since Polish Chassidim had a custom of announcing the next Rebbe immediately following *shivah,* Rav Meir, his son and newly crowned successor, sat with his Chassidim and drank a *le'chaim* to commemorate the occasion. The Chassidim brought him a very sharp whiskey with a high alcohol content, and he had a number of drinks. It was at that moment that he explained the concept of drinking a *le'chaim* following *shivah*.

"After a person dies, family members often second-guess themselves: 'What else could we have done to have changed the outcome, to have saved our loved one? Did we use the proper doctor? Should we have followed a different course of action?' Inevitably, they are racked with pain and guilt.

"These thoughts are heretic. The person's death was decreed on Rosh Hashanah. He died because *HaKadosh Baruch Hu* decided that it was his or her time to leave This Earth, and nothing could have prevented it.

"It is for this reason that we drink a *le'chaim* and make the blessing of '*Shehakol niheyeh bidvaro* — Through Whose word everything came to be.' This is a declaration in which we state that we realize everything happens for one reason: because Hashem wills it to happen, and He is the one Who orchestrates everything that takes place in this world.

"And then we drink a bit of whiskey to clear our minds of any heretic thoughts."

Rav Yechiel Michel Feinstein had a daughter who suffered from asthma. At times, she had terrible coughing fits, which she was unable to stop. At other times, she would wheeze or suffer from shortness of breath, and she needed an inhaler to clear her restricted passageways and allow her to breathe easier. The family members placed inhalers all over the house. This way, in case of an attack, there was always one handy.

One day, when she had an asthma attack, the family members ran to get an inhaler as they always did. But though they checked all the places where the inhalers were generally kept, not one could be found. The family panicked as the young girl was finding it more and more difficult to bring air to her lungs. They called Hatzalah and begged them to come and save the child. However, by the time the paramedics arrived, she was no longer breathing.

The family could not believe what had happened. Once more, they looked around the house. Within a few moments, all of the inhalers were found. In fact, there was one hidden under a bed, just a few feet away from where the girl had died.

The family was shattered and racked with feelings of guilt. Perhaps they should have had more inhalers around. Why hadn't they checked more often to make sure they were in their proper places? No matter how hard they tried to rationalize, they felt very guilty.

Hundreds of people came by during *shivah,* but the parents were inconsolable. They kept playing over the scene in their minds, again and again. When the great maggid, Rav Yaakov Galinsky, came to be *menachem avel,* he understood how guilt ridden they were. In order to give them the proper comfort, he repeated a thought he had heard from his rebbeim many years before.

"We know that we are supposed to do our *hishtadlus,* our bit of input. Hence, one should put forth effort to find a job, arrange a *shidduch,* or save himself from a dangerous situation. Yet that obligation is only what one must do from here on in. It is strictly forbidden to second-guess oneself and think that one could have done more and prevented a tragedy. Such thoughts are nothing but *apikorsus,* heresy."

He turned to the broken parents and spoke firmly. "I know that you are blaming yourselves that you did not put the inhalers in the proper places. Or perhaps you are placing the blame on those who were unable to find them when your daughter needed them most. But this tragedy came from Hashem. And it is He, and only He, Who is responsible for taking your daughter back."

The couple listened to the words of *nechamah*, as Rav Galinsky continued to encourage them, giving them the strength and hope they needed to move forward.

They realized that their job right now was to accept the difficult decree from Hashem, and that this acceptance would serve to elevate their daughter's *neshamah*.

Never Look Back

The following story dovetails beautifully with the previous one, further strengthening those who have suffered losses, to help them move forward — and not look back.

M

R. AND MRS. BERGILOFSKY WERE LIKE MANY OTHER couples living in Yerushalayim in the early 1950's. Alone in the world aside from each other, they struggled to find happiness and joy through perseverance and fortitude. Both of their families had been brutally murdered by the Nazis. Yet after all their suffering, the two of them managed to find each other. They shared each other's pain and committed to starting their lives over again.

But it was a lot easier said than done. After their modest wedding — attended only by friends, as neither had any relatives — they moved to Yerushalayim, hoping to leave the memories of the bloodshed of Europe behind. Though they spoke about how their children would rebuild the Jewish people, a number of years passed without the blessing of children in their home. They prayed and cried with all their might, until finally, they were blessed with a child.

Mordechai, who was named after his grandfather, was their entire universe. When he smiled at them for the first time, the world that was so dark finally had a beam of light shining on it. When he took his first steps, they danced with joy. And when he learned his first *pasuk* of *Chumash*, they rejoiced with tears.

Mordechai was his parents' dream. He excelled in his learning, and all of his teachers loved him dearly. When he finished eighth grade, he went on to a prestigious yeshivah, where his learning reached even greater heights. By the time he was 17, he was known as a *metzuyan* (excellent student), whose learning was matched only by his stellar character. Indeed, he was the light of their life.

What made him even more special was the fact that he was their only child. The Al-mighty had not blessed them with any more children, and so their lives continued to revolve exclusively around him. They doted on him and were extremely protective of where he went and what he did. Therefore, when he asked his parents if he could go swimming with his friends at the beach, they were a bit hesitant. But when he begged, they didn't have the heart to tell him no. Once granted permission, he waved goodbye and off he went.

They would never see him again.

Mordechai was a very good swimmer but a bit adventurous. He started swimming with his friends, but then he ventured out a bit too far. His friends were no more than 100 feet away when Mordechai slipped beneath the waves. The next thing they knew, he was gone. They swam over quickly, and frantically tried to find their friend, but to no avail. They finally did find his body, but that brought little comfort.

When the authorities came to the scene of the tragedy, his friends made sure to mention that Mordechai was an only child. The thought of breaking the news to his parents broke their hearts and they sobbed uncontrollably. As was to be expected, when Mordechai's parents received the horrific news, they both went completely numb. At first, they stared blankly at each other. *Could it possibly be? Would their Mordechai never be coming home again?*

The shock turned to unbearable agony. Their lives were over.

At the funeral, Mordechai's rebbeim spoke about his greatness in learning, his endearing personality, and what a wonderful son he was. Then they lamented about how unfortunate it was for an only child to be snatched away from his parents, after they had tried so valiantly to rebuild their lives. It was a gut-wrenching funeral; the tragedy was so great: truly beyond words.

Many people visited during *shivah*, yet the tone in the room was awkward and silent. No one had the words that could bring the proper comfort and solace. What was there to say? The Bergilofskys' lives had centered on their Mordechai. Now that he was gone, it was very hard for them to find purpose. How could they ever move forward?

Then Rav Yechiel Mordechai Gordon came to be *menachem avel*. He had endured tremendous suffering and loss in the Holocaust, yet he had rebuilt his life. With his great warmth and caring, he helped others rebuild, as well.

When Rav Yechiel Mordechai walked into the room, all were silent: the mourners and comforters alike. He sat down across from the bereaved couple and began speaking. The people in the room were now privy to one of the most faith-filled talks they would ever hear.

"As you may know, I, too, suffered terribly during the war. I lost my entire family and wondered how I would ever be able to rebuild. After much soul-searching, I came across the answer. And ever since then, I have not forgotten its message."

As he spoke, the couple listened attentively to his words, hoping to find something to hold onto, something they could grasp that would lessen their pain.

"In life, when tragedies happen, we must always hold onto one thought: Never look back. What has happened has happened. It won't help to question why. And in truth, there really is nothing that can be done about the past. All we can do is move forward. That is what has kept me going throughout these years. I never looked back. I only looked to the future: to hope, and to possible comfort."

Never look back.

Those three words, and the simplistic but profound lesson conveyed within them, were the only words that would bring comfort to the Bergilofskys. It helped them accept the harsh decree and enabled them to deal with the loss of their beloved son.

And though they always felt a void in their lives, they were able to move forward, with the hope that tomorrow would be a brighter day.

TO FREE THE IMPRISONED

I N THE LATE 1970'S, THERE WAS GREAT POLITICAL UNREST IN Iran following the overthrow of the leader known as the Shah. Thousands of Jews fled for their lives. Through the considerable efforts of tireless *askanim*, especially Rabbi Naftali Herman Neuberger of Yeshivas Ner Yisroel, many Iranian Jews were able to escape.

During this time of upheaval, a young woman from Iran arrived in Israel. Her husband, however, had gotten caught up in the Iranian revolution and converted to Islam. Not only did he refuse to give her a divorce, he didn't believe in the idea entirely. Her situation appeared to be beyond hope. How in the world would a Jewish court of law be able to influence a man who had converted to Islam?

Rav Mordechai Eliyahu, the chief rabbi of Israel at the time, received a letter from the woman. Included was the documentation of her court appearances and her husband's refusals to give a divorce. Rav Mordechai did not hesitate for a second. He took out official Israeli stationery and composed a letter to Rav Yedidyah Shofet, who was still living in Iran.

When the envelope stamped with the official Israeli seal reached Iran, the Iranian officials brought it to the censorship committee. The translator revealed that the letter included information about the Iranian leader Ayatollah Khomeini. Within a short while, the mysterious letter was brought before the Ayatollah himself.

In the letter, Rav Eliyahu relayed the woman's story and then made a seemingly ridiculous request. He asked Rav Shofet to go before the Ayatollah and say that since he is a deeply religious man, Khomeini should help a young woman who is prevented by religious law from remarrying. He hoped that he would be sympathetic to their cause.

Intrigued by the letter and flattered by the compliment, the leader of the Iranian revolution decided that he was going to facilitate a divorce for this woman whose husband had converted to Islam. To that end, he summoned Rav Shofet to the palace. Rav Shofet was no fool. He knew that if somebody was summoned to the palace, he would most likely not return. With tears streaming down his face, he gave his family members final instructions. He put his burial shrouds under his clothing, and he handed his will to his children. And then, escorted by the soldiers of the Revolutionary Guard, he made his way to the palace.

He stood before the Ayatollah, who asked him, "Do you know someone named Rav Mordechai Eliyahu?" Rav Shofet had no idea where the conversation was heading. He didn't know if he should admit to knowing the chief rabbi, or if such acknowledgment was dangerous. He decided to admit to the truth and pray for the best.

The Ayatollah then asked, "Do you listen to this rabbi?" Rav Shofet once again answered in the affirmative. Khomeini then said, "Well, take a look at what the rabbi wrote about me." He was flattered that the rav had acknowledged that he was a G-d-fearing man and that he would do what was right.

Then the Ayatollah asked Rav Shofet, "So what must we do to convince this fellow to give a divorce to his wife?" Although the situation was bizarre, Rav Shofet sensed that the hands of the Almighty were guiding him in this interaction. Rav Shofet proceeded to give a synopsis of the Jewish laws of divorce and explained that it was necessary for the husband to agree to give the divorce, and that he not be forced to do so against his will.

The Ayatollah instructed his guards to bring the husband before him. The husband stood before the Ayatollah, trembling in fear. The Ayatollah told him in no uncertain terms that he must give his wife a divorce immediately, and then he turned to his guards. "If he does not agree to give his wife a divorce, break all of his bones."

He turned to the rabbi and said, "I apologize. It is people like this who give us a bad name and make the world think that we are not good people." Rav Shofet tried his best to keep a smirk off his face. Who knew if he would be next to receive a censure?

Rav Shofet explained very gently that the husband cannot be forced to give the divorce: he must give it willingly. The Ayatollah understood and asked for a few moments to *explain* to the husband the importance of giving the divorce willingly.

Obviously, it didn't take more than a few seconds for the husband to understand that if he valued his life, he would have to give the divorce — and he would have to do so willingly. As soon as the husband agreed, Rav Shofet received permission to place a call from the Ayatollah's palace to the Jewish community in France. From there, they relayed the message to the office of the chief rabbi, detailing the story, along with instructions about how to handle the divorce.

Rav Shofet accepted the divorce on behalf of the wife. Miraculously, a woman who thought she would be a prisoner forever was freed.

At times, we feel trapped in an endless stream of frustration and heartache, yet nothing is impossible for the Al-mighty. We, hindered by our human limitations, must still do our utmost to help others — while leaving the rest in His hands.

We often find that anything can happen. Even that which is beyond our wildest imagination.

ALWAYS HAVE A CHANCE

ONE OF THE PERKS OF TRAVELING FOR SPEAKING engagements is the unique opportunity to meet some wonderful people from around the globe. On a recent trip to Manchester, England, I had the privilege of staying at the home of Rav Moshe Kupitz and his rebbetzin, the children of the Manchester rosh yeshivah, Rav Yehudah Zev Segal. They were warm, kind, and hospitable. Although they offered me supper, I had just eaten so I had to refuse. But Rav Moshe said, "I have something that you won't be able to turn down: a great story!" He was right.

Rav Moshe's son lives in Eretz Yisrael and delivers a *shiur* to a group of semiretired American *baalebatim* (working men). Recently, they finished a *masechta* and decided to celebrate with a lavish *siyum*. At the *siyum*, one of the participants had a *le'chaim* or two and decided to share a fascinating story: his own.

After surviving the war, my parents had nothing left to their name, and they wanted nothing to do with Judaism. I didn't even have a bar mitzvah. The only thing Jewish in our home was the language; Yiddish is my mother tongue.

Unfortunately, as I grew older, I began to hang out with some of the boys in the neighborhood who were not the best of influences. Before long, I was dealing with illegal contraband and making a lot of money. One night, I had a meeting in a restaurant with some "big shots." The meeting turned out to be a sting operation run by the FBI. By the end of the evening, in which all the incriminating conversation had been recorded, I and two buddies found ourselves in handcuffs.

One of the other men arrested was able to escape. The second agreed to exchange information for a lighter sentence, so I was left holding the "bag." I was facing a sentence of 25 years in prison, and I didn't know what to do. As soon as I posted bail, I went to one of the best lawyers in Manhattan. After agreeing to pay tens of thousands of dollars, I was told that he could try to get me off — but it did not look good.

I left his office despondent and broken. I walked all the way down to the Lower East Side, until I came to a coffee shop. Upon seeing me crying over my coffee, a man approached me and asked, in a heavy European accent, "Vat's your problem?"

I replied, "What do you know about problems?" In response, the man rolled up his sleeve and showed me the numbers on his arm. In a very deliberate tone, he told me, "I know all about problems. You tell me vat your problem is."

Feeling a bit more reassured, I told him the entire story. When I finished, he responded, "You don't need a lawyer; vat you need is a Rebbe! Come vit me and I vill take you to a Rebbe." We walked a few blocks and then went up six flights of stairs to the apartment of the Skolya Rebbe. Since I knew Yiddish, I was able to tell my story to the Rebbe, and I cried bitterly as I shared my plight. When I had finished pouring out my heart, he told me, "Don't worry about a thing. Show up in court, and your lawyer will come late. But don't be nervous, since you will win the court case."

And so it was. The day arrived; the court appearance was set for 9 a.m. The FBI agents were all there and the lawyer didn't show. I was beyond nervous. Finally, the clerks called the lawyer and asked him where he was. He apologized and explained that he was stuck out of town and would not be able to make it. He said he was sending a replacement.

My heart was beating wildly and I felt faint. I couldn't believe it. My life was hanging in the balance and he was sending a replacement?!

At 10 o'clock, a 22-year-old lawyer walked into the courtroom. I nearly passed out. It was clear that he was very new at this work and very inexperienced. He brought in some papers, put down his briefcase, and before long the trial was underway. The prosecution presented a flawless case against me. As they played over the recording, it was clear to me and everyone else in that courtroom that I was guilty. Looking at the judge's face, I could tell that he agreed.

Then my lawyer had his opportunity to present my defense. It didn't take long, and there wasn't much to say; it was fairly obvious what the verdict would be. The judge went into his chamber and emerged a few minutes later. With my hands covering my face and tears in my eyes, I braced myself for the worst. However, to the amazement of everyone present, he began to criticize everything the prosecution had said. He found fault in their presentation and holes in their logic; the prosecutors' faces fell. After a few moments, the judge banged his gavel and declared my innocence.

I was completely overwhelmed. Tears were streaming down my face as I congratulated the rookie lawyer for getting me off. He smiled sheepishly and admitted that it was his first case.

Now I was completely astounded. I asked him how he thought he could win this case when the evidence was overwhelmingly in favor of the prosecution.

He smiled, shrugged his shoulders, and quipped, "You see the judge? He's my grandpa."

Thrilled at the turn of events, I ran back to the Rebbe and excitedly told him that I was free. I asked him how he had known how things would turn out, and he told me, "How I knew is irrelevant, but I do know that when someone does you a favor, you should do a favor in return."

I pulled out my checkbook, ready to write a check for whatever amount he asked. But he told me to put away the checkbook; he didn't want my money. He had one favor to ask of me. He wanted me to put on tefillin every day. He didn't ask for Shabbos and he didn't ask for kosher. That was his one and only request.

Of course, I readily agreed and headed out to purchase a pair of tefillin. I handed the Rebbe's note of recommendation to Rabbi Jacobson of Crown Heights, and he sold me a pair.

"That was many years ago," he concluded, "and here I am today. I am a Torah-observant Jew, blessed with a magnificent family."

With all the challenges we face, no matter how incriminating the evidence may be against us, the judge is our Grandpa. Therefore, though it seems that the collective redemption of the Jewish people and the personal salvation of each individual in crisis is a far-fetched dream, we always have a chance.

Our Grandpa can redeem us at any time.

TO AWAKEN
A SLEEPING GIANT

On Thursday, June 12, 2014, three yeshivah boys were abducted by Arabs from the Alon Shvut Junction in Israel. After Klal Yisrael spent 18 days praying and searching, the boys were found: murdered. The tragedy prompted the following article.

OUR BOYS WILL NEVER BE COMING HOME.
I just heard the heartbreaking news a few moments ago. Who isn't crying today? There will be people calling for revenge against the cursed Arabs and their subhuman terrorist groups. Indeed, the *Keil Nekamos* (G-d of Vengeance) will see to it that they receive their deserved punishment. But what about us? Where do we go from here?

I was given the daunting task of speaking to the boys of Camp Dora Golding, where I am a division head, and breaking the news to them. This forced me to contemplate the lessons we can take from this tragedy. I am not that naïve to think that these are *the* messages we should take. Rather, the following are some of the disorganized, spontaneous thoughts of a shaken fellow Yid:

1. We all feel like crying. Most of us have shed tears today. Indeed, we should not hold back. The Chasam Sofer writes that the tears we shed after someone is taken from our midst are like the *nesachim*, water libations, that accompany the sacrifices brought in the *Beis HaMikdash*. Our tears complete the *korban* (sacrifice). The tears we shed today for these three *korbanos* are *nesachim,* as well.

2. No Jewish prayer goes unanswered. We may wonder: What happened to the millions of *kapitlach* (chapters) of *Tehillim* recited over the past few weeks? Nearly 20 years ago, Nachshon Wachsman, *Hy"d*, an Israeli soldier, was kidnapped by a group of terrorists. Klal Yisrael stormed the gates of Heaven. Women lit their Shabbos candles extra early. Tens of thousands gathered at the Kosel for a special *yom tefillah* (day of supplication). Despite all of this, in a daring and valiant rescue attempt by the Israeli army in which the terrorists were killed, Nachshon did not survive. In an unforgettable interview, a reporter asked Nachshon's father why

G-d ignored all the prayers. Why hadn't He listened? Mr. Wachsman's answer was epic: "Indeed, Hashem listened and answered. But the answer was *no*."

3. Hashem loves us. Recently, a 13-year-old *yasom* (orphan) told me something very powerful. During the last few days of his mother's life, he asked his father, "When is Mommy going to get better?" His father replied, "Hashem loves Mommy, and if He wants her to get better, she will; and if He doesn't want her to get better, she won't. But always remember, Hashem loves Mommy." For reasons we will never understand, Hashem wanted to bring these three special *neshamos* (souls) closer to Him in *Shamayim* (Heaven). But Hashem loves Eyal, Naftali, and Gil-Ad. And He loves their families, friends, and anyone else who is pained by their death. It is crucial for children to know that even when it is difficult to feel the love, Hashem always loves us.

4. We must remain united. Our hearts are shattered, but we became one. Over the past 18 days, we have united in an unprecedented display of *achdus* (unity). Jews of all stripes joined as brothers, hand in hand, waiting with bated breath to hear some good news, and because of it, we have all grown in some way. Yair Lapid visited the home of one of the captives and assured the boy's mother that he had rummaged through his home searching for his grandfather's *siddur*. Upon hearing the news, he felt moved to pray for the first time in six years. Who could have ever imagined? *Achdus* stirred his soul.

It has stirred our collective souls.

The yearning and hopeful song of *Acheinu kol Beis Yisrael* (our Jewish brothers) could be heard reverberating throughout the vast landscape of Torah Jewry.

From Yeshivat Gush Etzion to Yeshivas Ponovezh.

From Chassidishe *shtieblach* to Young Israels.

Klal Yisrael became one.

The way we were meant to be.

Ke'ish echad be'leiv echad (Like one man with one heart).

This was a stunning turnaround from the crippling fragmentation we experienced a few months before. And now, with the tragic deaths of Eyal, Naftali, and Gil-Ad, all our hearts are shattered.

But we must not let our unity become shattered, as well. Look how a tragedy allowed us to put aside our differences. Look how it made us grow.

To summarize the words of Naftali Frankel's mother, "Taking our children has not broken us. It has united us in ways thought impossible a few short months ago."

Hamas has awakened the sleeping giant that is the *achdus* of Klal Yisrael.

Let it never sleep again.

OF PICTURES AND APARTMENTS

The following story is in the sefer LeHisadein BeAhavasecha. It teaches that even when we are convinced that things are as we see them, often the very opposite is true.

ONE MORNING, MORDY DINGMAN WAS IN HIS CAR, ON his way to the early-morning *minyan*. Even though it was Sunday, he had a lot going on at his business that day and was eager to get an early start. As he was driving, his phone rang. When he picked it up, he received some very upsetting news. His landlord told him that he expected him to be out of his apartment within the next two months. He was selling the building to a developer, who was planning on knocking it down. Mordy and his wife had been living there for 17 years, and it was not easy to find another apartment. What a disappointing start to his day! Unfortunately, this was only the beginning. Things would get much worse!

After he finished davening, instead of driving straight to work, he decided to go home and tell his wife the news. As he drove, his mind raced. Where would they move? Would they enjoy the same relationship with their new neighbors? Where would he daven? As he drove past the houses in the neighborhood, he couldn't help but look at each one and wonder if that was going to be his next home.

As he let his mind wander, he suddenly realized that the light was turning red. He slammed on the brakes, but his car skidded. The harder he pressed on the brakes, the more he lost control. It all happened in a matter of seconds. Before he knew it, his car ran into an elderly couple who was crossing the street on their way home from their Sunday religious services. As he did so, he caught a glimpse of the terrified looks on the old couple's faces. Seconds later, his car slammed into a pole and finally came to a stop.

Although Mordy was banged up, he did not lose consciousness. The door on the driver's side was smashed in, so he crawled out of the other door. He realized that his arm was broken, as were some of his ribs, but he felt fortunate that it was not worse. However, soon he realized the awful consequences of his accident. The elderly couple was dead; they had been killed instantly.

The police sorted out the paperwork, and an ambulance brought Mordy to the hospital. They examined him carefully, and after casting his arm and bandaging him up, they released him. A few days later, though, the police informed him that he was being charged with vehicular manslaughter. Witnesses said that he had skidded right through the red light, and he should have been more careful.

A few weeks later, Mordy was taken to trial. The prosecution presented its case. The lawyer was thorough in his presentation.

The evidence was overwhelmingly against Mordy. It seemed fairly certain that the judge was going to rule against him.

Then the defense discovered that an oil rig had spilled its load a few days earlier on that very spot. Hence, the road was slick, even though it was a sunny morning. This last-minute defense carried the day. To Mordy's immense relief, the judge dismissed the case and declared Mordy free of all charges.

Although Mordy knew that he was officially innocent, the feelings of guilt still hung over him and tormented him night and day. He was responsible for the deaths of two innocent people, and there was nothing he could do about the situation. He stopped eating and rarely smiled. He didn't even go to work.

Looking for encouragement, he wrote a letter to Rav Chaim Kanievsky, in which he described the events. As is his wont, Rav Chaim's reply was short and to the point. It was a cryptic, one-word response: "Amalek!" Mordy had no idea how to react. He showed the response to others, but nobody could figure it out.

In the meantime, he still had not found a place to live, and in one week he was going to be evicted from his apartment. One day, the real-estate agent called and told him about an apartment that had just been put on the market, which was too good an opportunity to pass up. Mordy and his wife went to the address the agent had given them; it was not far from their former neighborhood, which was a start. As they looked around the apartment, they actually liked what they saw.

Mordy looked at the photographs of the former residents, and he knew he recognized the faces from somewhere. And then, he froze in his tracks. It was the couple he had killed. He could never forget their faces.

Mordy sat down so he could catch his breath. After a few moments, on a hunch, he opened a desk drawer. Inside, there was another picture of the old man. But this time, the man was much younger and looked different. He was dressed in a soldier's uniform.

A Nazi soldier's uniform.

Underneath, in big letters, were the words: Treblinka, 1942.

Mordy finally understood Rav Chaim's cryptic message. He was telling him not to feel guilty about the accident, because the man he had killed had been a soldier in a death camp that had taken the lives of 850,000 Jews.

And among those 850,000 were Mordy's grandparents, aunts, uncles, and cousins. Over 50 people in his family had been killed in Treblinka.

Somehow, this elderly Nazi couple had escaped the watchful eyes of Nazi hunters.

Tears came to his eyes, as he finally felt comforted. What he thought was a careless act of manslaughter was, in truth, the Almighty's way of making things right.

This volume is part of
THE ARTSCROLL® SERIES
an ongoing project of
translations, commentaries and expositions on
Scripture, Mishnah, Talmud, Midrash, Halachah,
liturgy, history, the classic Rabbinic writings,
biographies and thought.

For a brochure of current publications
visit your local Hebrew bookseller
or contact the publisher:

Mesorah Publications, ltd.

4401 Second Avenue
Brooklyn, New York 11232
(718) 921-9000
www.artscroll.com